We work with leading authors to develop the strongest educational materials in law, bringing cutting-edge thinking and best learning practice to a global market.

Under a range of well-known imprints, including Prentice Hall, we craft high quality print and electronic publications which help readers to understand and apply their content, whether studying or at work.

To find out more about the complete range of our publishing, please visit us on the World Wide Web at: *www.pearsoneduc.com*

LAW ON THE WEB
A Guide for Students and Practitioners

Stuart Stein

Prentice
Hall

An imprint of **Pearson Education**

Harlow, England • London • New York • Boston • San Francisco • Toronto
Sydney • Tokyo • Singapore • Hong Kong • Seoul • Taipei • New Delhi
Cape Town • Madrid • Mexico City • Amsterdam • Munich • Paris • Milan

Pearson Education Limited
Edinburgh Gate
Harlow
Essex CM20 2JE
England

and Associated Companies throughout the world

Visit us on the World Wide Web at:
www.pearsoneduc.com

First published 2003

ISBN 0130 60571 9

British Library Cataloguing-in-Publication Data
A catalogue record for this book is available from the British Library

10 9 8 7 6 5 4 3 2 1
07 06 05 04 03

Typeset in 9/13pt Stone serif by 35
Printed in Great Britain by Henry Ling Ltd., at the Dorset Press, Dorchester, Dorset

Contents

Preface

This book is aimed at students and academic staff whose recourse to Internet-based resources is likely to be essentially pragmatic. The questions that they are likely to be interested in include the following.

- 'What resources are available?'

- 'How can I find them most efficiently?'

- 'How do I locate potentially useful mailing lists that deal with the particular subjects that I am interested in?'

- 'How do I manage participation in such forums, such as subscribing, unsubscribing, retaining anonymity, receiving weekly digests rather than daily messages, or switching them off temporarily?'

- 'Which are the primary Web sites dealing with my subject specialisations and interests?'

- 'How do I reference Internet materials?'

- 'Under what circumstances should I refer to a subject directory or a search engine?'

- 'What search syntax should I employ in order not to have to sift through thousands of records?'

- 'How can I track down a resource that I found earlier but which cannot be accessed from the same Web address subsequently?'

These are some of the questions that are addressed in this book. It is not aimed, therefore, at students or staff who wish to become experts on all matters associated with the Internet and its varied forums, although it does provide a useful foundation for those who would wish to do so. Throughout I have assumed that most students and academic staff who will want to exploit the uses of the Internet will wish to do so in order to accomplish more efficiently their primary interests in teaching, learning, and researching. It is entirely feasible to track down subject-specific materials, manage participation on mailing lists, and reduce search times significantly without becoming an Internet expert. Unless you are using the Internet for leisure purposes, the objective should be to be in and out as quickly and effortlessly as possible.

Part I focuses on the Internet address scheme and the referencing of resources. Many users fail to appreciate that Internet addresses, or URLs, provide information that can be very useful in identifying the sources of the Web pages that they have downloaded. This may be of relevance to assessing the authoritativeness of their compilers. They may also provide clues to finding those pages that have been relocated to other parts of the server on which they were originally stored, or to other servers, either within the same or another organisation. As for the accurate referencing of Internet resources, this is increasingly as much an integral part of academic work as is that of printed sources.

Part II focuses on the development of search skills. After a review of Internet indexing systems and subject directories, I explore briefly the workings of search engines and then concentrate on the development of basic and advanced searching techniques using them. There are now hundreds of different types of search engine available. Typing in a word and returning a list of records that meet the query syntax is not difficult. What does require some experience and knowledge is that of compiling queries that filter out unwanted records. The volume of information accessible over the Internet, in conjunction with the way in which search engines parse files, can result in simple queries returning links to hundreds of thousands, sometimes millions, of documents that match the search syntax employed. No one has the time or the mental energy to sift through all this. If you construct your query carefully you should be able in many instances to ensure that the information that you require is included in the first 20 or 30 records returned. If not, as I argue later, you should construct a different query. With experience and some experimentation you should narrow this down to the first ten. Experts can narrow it down to three. Anyone who works their way through these chapters can become quite expert. The savings in time will be considerable, and you should be able to locate pages that otherwise you might only have come across by chance. Chapter 7 in Part II tackles basic information relating to the location of mailing lists dealing with particular subjects, and how to use them most effectively. Mailing lists are valuable sources of information on many issues, as well as useful research sampling frames in some instances.

Part III is an annotated guide to law resources. These do not exhaust those available on publicly accessible Internet sites. I have focused on those that I think that most readers will find particularly useful. These are sites that, unless otherwise specified, provide useful topic-related information. I do not generally include sites that merely include a long list of non-annotated Internet addresses. Many of these, when followed through, do not provide much of substance; sometimes only more lists of URLs. Also, I do not include resources where it is impossible to identify who the compilers are, where they appear not to be updated regularly, where the pages are sloppily compiled, in relation to both the underlying HTML coding and the substantive topic. Too many academics have seen fit to contribute to a form of Internet pollution, uploading PowerPoint slide materials, or summary lecture notes, that they have provided in some lecturing or paper presentation context. These are generally of little use unless you actually attended the presentation. Even then, you would need a good memory or have to refer to notes taken. I also endeavour to focus on sites that are likely to be around for some time. If the site consists of two or three files which have been there for some time, it is less likely, in my experience, to be updated, or to remain there permanently, than a site which has hundreds of files, and is linked to the main subject interests of an individual or to the objectives of a major organisation.

Because some of the URLs are lengthy, and as these sometimes change over time, to the right of each that is listed in Chapter 9, you will find a number in brackets, e.g. *http://www.icrc.org/*(57). At *http://www.booksites.net/stein*, on the publisher's Web site, you will find a complete list of the URLs, numbered sequentially. To save the typing in of the URLs, something that is always subject to typing errors, you can do one of two things. Download that page and click on the URL whose associated page you want to access. Don't forget to bookmark this page so that you do not have to type in the address subsequently. Alternatively, save that page to disk, either floppy or on your PC. When you want to access any of the sites listed, open your browser and load the page from your disk. Now select the URL of the site you are interested in. When you want to access other sites on the list, use the back navigation button, the drop-down arrow to the right of it or the address box of the browser. The URLs will be amended from time to time if necessary and the pages at the publisher's site changed accordingly. The publisher's Web site will also provide updated advice relating to basic and advanced searches in AltaVista arising from recent additions to its functionality.

In Part IV I provide some information on how to construct basic Web pages, and on miscellaneous skills and configuration issues relevant to a more proficient management of Internet-related work.

About the author

Dr Stuart Stein is a Visiting Fellow at the University of the West of England, where he has taught courses on sociology, social psychology, comparative genocide, and human rights. He has extensive experience in the use of information technologies for the delivery of educational materials, and is the Director of the Web Genocide Documentation Centre.

Dr Stein is the author of *Learning, Teaching and Researching on the Internet*, has written extensively on electronic pedagogy, writes on genocide, and is currently writing a book on the management of war crimes. He is also the author of *Psychology on the Web, Politics on the Web*, and *Sociology on the Web*, published by Prentice Hall, an imprint of Pearson Education.

Acknowledgements

We are grateful to the following for permission to reproduce copyright material:

Figures 5.1, 5.2 and 6.1 reproduced from screenshots from AltaVista® websites, *www.altavista.com*, or *www.uk.altavista.com*, AltaVista Internet Operations Limited, Copyright © 2002 AltaVista Company, reproduced with the permission of AltaVista Internet Operations Limited. All rights reserved; Figure 6.2 reproduced from screenshot from *www.google.com*, Copyright © 2002 Google, Inc., reproduced with the permission of Google, Inc.; Figures 10.1, 10.3, 10.4, 10.5, 12.4 and 12.5 reproduced from screenshots from *Netscape Navigator 6.0*, and from *http://wp.netscape.com/*, Netscape website, Copyright © 2002 Netscape Communications Corporation, screenshots used with permission; Figure 10.6 reproduced from table from *www.netpanel.com/features/internet/times.htm*, *net*panel, Copyright © 2002 Michael Yigdall and Jonathan Strine; Figures 10.7, 12.1, 12.2, 12.3, 12.6, 12.7, 12.8, 12.9 reproduced from screenshots of Microsoft® Internet Explorer 6.0, *www.microsoft.com*, Copyright © 1995–2001 Microsoft Corporation. Screen shots reprinted by permission from Microsoft Corporation.

In some instances we have been unable to trace the owners of copyright material, and we would appreciate any information that would enable us to do so.

Part I

WEB RESOURCES

1

Introductory glossary

When I wrote *Learning, Teaching and Researching on the Internet*, in 1998, a very significant proportion of the undergraduate students that I taught, and many academic staff, were relatively unfamiliar with the Internet, the Web, and the files and interactive forums that were publicly accessible to them over their own Internet-linked PCs, or educational networks. Accordingly, I included separate chapters detailing the structure of the Internet and how to use Web browsers. This has now become largely unnecessary. Nearly all new undergraduate students have had experience of using the Internet from schools, and many of these have also had Internet access at home. University academic staffs, through a variety of institutional programmes, as well as through targeted grants provided by higher educational funding councils, are equally familiar with the rudiments of Internet structure and the use of Web browsers.

Nonetheless, there are always some terms that it is not always easy to conjure up from memory, or even that one desires to store there, but that are necessary for the narratives that follow. Accordingly, and in order not to clutter up the text with definitional issues, some of the more central terms are defined here as well as in the Glossary at the end of this book. The meanings that you impute to some of these terms (e.g. Web pages/pages) may differ from those that I employ. Before proceeding, cast a quick glance over them to see what is available and, perhaps, brush up on one or two that have slipped from memory, or that are unfamiliar.

Anonymous users Refers to a specific category of user, one who is entitled to access all, or particular files on an Internet-connected server. Generally, anonymous access rights are granted by Web server administrators so that anyone who has access to a Web browser can access files on the machine in question by keying in the appropriate URL (see definition below). It is a means of making files publicly available.

Client The software application that resides on the PC or network of the user that is used in order to request information or processing of data from a server (see definition below).

Explorer The name of the Microsoft operating system's file management application. It is accessible from the *Programs* option on the *Start* menu.

Hits Refers to the number of entries included in a database that relate to the query entered by the user searching it.

Home Page Generally used to refer to the introductory page of a Web presentation, the one to which all other pages are linked, which, in turn, ordinarily link back to it.

HTML (Hypertext Markup Language) A structural mark-up language that indicates to specialised software applications that can *read* it, how the text, graphic images, and video and audio files associated with it are to be displayed. HTML is concerned principally with the structure of documents, rather than with their appearance.

Internet Service Provider Generic term that covers private companies providing Internet connectivity and additional online services to users, usually in return for a monthly subscription fee.

Publicly accessible Here refers to files that can be accessed without having to pay fees, and excludes those that are available only to persons who have access to particular networks of organisations, whether commercial, military, governmental, or other.

Search engine A tool for interrogating a database of information relating to electronically accessible resources (files).

Server/Web server A term for the computer that *serves up* files to those entitled to have access to them when a request is made through a *client* application.

URL (Uniform Resource Locator) An Internet address. These have standardised formats. The URL specifies the type of Internet service that is being accessed (World Wide Web, FTP, etc.), and the file path of the resource being sought. The URL is the entry that is inserted in the location/go box in a browser.

Web pages/Web files Strictly speaking, a Web page is the file that appears in the browser window when an URL/Web address is accessed. These pages may be in varying formats. Some of them are Web pages in the strict meaning of the term, that is, pages that are written in HTML, i.e. Hypertext Markup Language. Many, however, are written in other formats, including Word documents (.doc extension), Portable Document Format (.pdf), or Text (.txt). In fact, referencing *pages* in this context is misleading, as what is being accessed is a file. A Web page is an HTML file, with the suffix .htm, .html, or .shtml. These may include links to other files, such as graphic files, which are downloaded at about the same time.

When I employ the term Web page/s or page/s, I mean to refer to *files*, which may, or may not, be HTML files. There are many files that can be accessed over the Internet that cannot be displayed in a Web browser, although they may be downloaded through its use (e.g. software applications).

2

Web addresses:
what's in a URL?

Internet addresses enable the downloading of required files, and are important tools for assisting in identifying certain characteristics of the individuals and organisations that upload them. They can also be useful for tracking down files that have been relocated, and identifying their authors, this frequently being the only assist to tracking their current Internet locations, if any. As a common reason for being unable to access a particular file is that the author of the link has mistyped the address, knowledge of how addresses should be compiled, or are likely to be structured, permits rectification of errors and access to files erroneously referenced.

Understandably, many Web authors are not especially Internet or Web savvy. Their objective is to get their messages across. These are frequently uploaded in the form of a series of Web files (pages), constituting a Web site (presentation). The pages, with the exception of the Home, or entry page, may carry little information other than the contents, as their authors appear to assume that those accessing any part of the presentation will enter through the front door, as it were.

Most of those accessing pages, however, will do so following the submission of a query to a search engine. These do not distinguish between Home and other pages. So, when someone accesses pages other than the Home page, they may have very little information to go on as to who owns the site, who authored the page, and where the related pages, if any, are. Sometimes there are navigational aids in the form of links to a Home page or an email address. Too often, there are not.

Here is one illustration. In searching for resources on Pavlovian conditioning, I came across a link, via a search engine, to ***http://highered.mcgraw-hill.com/ olc/dl/27748/kle90462_ch03.pdf.*** This is a 44-page PDF file entitled Principles and Applications of Pavlovian Conditioning. No author is mentioned. From browsing the contents I concluded that this was a scholarly discussion of the subject. On the first page it was indicated that this was Chapter 3; therefore, part of a book, the rest of which could also be online. However, as no author was mentioned, it would be impossible to reference it, doubts would remain about its authority, and as there were no navigational aids, it was not possible to establish whether other chapters were available online, although experience and examination of the URL suggested to me that they would not be. The URL, or address, was the only navigational aid available, and it provided me with answers to these questions, as illustrated below.

URLs, pronounced Earl or U R L, are Internet addresses, not just Web addresses. URL denotes Uniform Resource Locator. URLs reference the location of files of all types that are accessible from computers that are connected to the networked infrastructure that we refer to as the Internet. A URL is the virtual equivalent of the postal address or telephone number. It needs to be inserted in an Internet-related software application, such as a browser, in order to download the file that it references. In what follows I will be referring only to some files, namely, Web pages.

Just as substantial numbers of people and families change their geographical location, a very significant number of files stored on Internet-linked servers move virtually, in the sense that they have a different URL or address. Important differences exist between the components of this analogy.

- Knowledge of a postal address, or a phone number, provides very little information about the person whose address or phone number it is, other than geographical location, which might be associated with other variables, such as socio-economic status. Knowledge of the URL invariably provides more detail.

- Knowledge about the occupant associated with a particular postal address does not provide much information about their subsequent location if they have moved, although the occupant might still be contactable through possession of allied information. Knowledge of the URL, coupled with information concerning the content and structure of the Web page, and, if available, details of the author, makes it feasible to establish relatively quickly where the page has moved to if it is still available.

- The Web files that users wish to locate are situated on Internet-linked computers. Although from some vantage points virtual space is enormous in size and cannot be mapped accurately due to the volume of daily additions and changes, it is frequently significantly easier to track particular files with the aid of search tools and directories than it is to locate persons from a very substantially smaller population pool in geographical space.

Everyone who uses the Internet encounters dead URLs within a very short space of time. They are so common that many users just move on to something else. If the user is exploring for pleasure, and/or there are many alternative sources accessible, this is just a minor irritant. If, on the other hand, the objective is to locate a file that is needed for some particular objective, or a particular file, especially when it has been accessed previously at the location addressed, irritation is compounded.

Frequently, all is not lost. The URL that does not deliver, along with other information that we may be able to glean from our past knowledge of the file, if we have any, or a search engine entry, may provide a reasonable basis for locating it if it is still accessible. It should be noted, however, that while some files are given different virtual addresses, with or without physical relocation, other files are permanently deleted.

The structure of a URL

Files on a Web server are organised very much like they are on a stand-alone PC, or on network file servers. The majority of users of stand-alone PCs have one hard disk, or drive, invariably referred to as the *c:\ drive*. That drive is sub-divided into various directories and sub-directories (folders), as in Figure 2.1. Assume that in the *Articles pdf* directory we have a file called *about.pdf*. The reference for that file would be: *c:\Articles pdf\about.pdf* signifying that the file *about.pdf* was located in the *Articles pdf* directory on the *c:* drive. Similarly, if there were an article in the *Armenia* sub-directory called *geography.doc*, its reference would be *c:\capture\Armenia\geography.doc* signifying that it was located in the *Armenia* directory of the *capture* directory, on the *c:* drive. As you move down the directory tree, you add more backward slashes, \. (*Note:* the terms directory and folder are used interchangeably in this context.)

Figure 2.2 is a graphic of some of the directories on one of the Web sites that I have created. The top, or root, directory is ***http://www.ess.uwe.ac.uk***, which is recognisable as part of a URL, or Internet address. The *www.ess.uwe.ac.uk* component is the equivalent of the *c:* component of the file location in my earlier example. What this portion denotes, or points to, is this particular

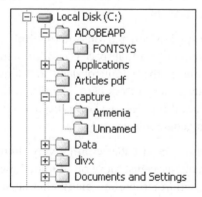

Figure 2.1

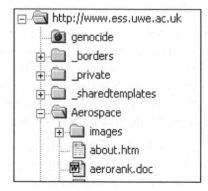

Figure 2.2

computer on the Internet. When you enter a URL that does not have directories, such as *http://www.microsoft.co.uk*, what you access is the *Home page*, referred to also as the *root* or *Index* file of the Web server whose address is indicated.

The *http://* component indicates that the file is on a Web server, http denoting Hypertext Transfer Protocol. The machine on which the Web site is located in this example also has an associated FTP server, which is designated *ftp://www.ess.uwe.ac.uk*, signifying that in requesting files from it you will be using the FTP, or File Transfer Protocol, to do so. The separate segments of file paths on Web servers, that is, the route to the file, are split by forward slashes, in contrast to backward slashes on a stand-alone PC.

From Figure 2.2 you can see that in the *Aerospace* directory, there is a file named *about.htm*. To send a request from a browser to download this file you would enter the URL *http://www.ess.uwe.ac.uk/Aerospace/about.htm* to indicate that the file was located on the computer *www.ess.uwe.ac.uk*, in the *Aerospace* directory, and that it was a Web page. As the file that is being requested has the suffix *htm* this signifies that it is an HTML file, or Web page. As the protocol is *http*, this indicates that that protocol is being used to request it.

In sum, *http://www.ess.uwe.ac.uk/Aerospace/about.htm*, a fairly typical URL in structure, tells us two things. The *www.ess.uwe.ac.uk* component, known as the *domain name* component, locates the specific computer on the Internet. *Aerospace* locates the place (directory) on that computer where the document that we are interested in, *about.htm*, is located. The last component, *about.htm*, is the most important from the point of view of the person trying to locate it, but the other components are essential to track down this particular document, as there are probably hundreds of thousands of documents, if not millions, with the file name *about.htm*, just as there are many entries for Smith in address and telephone directories in the UK and other English-speaking countries.

The domain name *www.ess.uwe.ac.uk* is in fact a mnemonic. It corresponds to the IP address, IP standing for Internet Protocol, 164.11.32.97. Every domain name corresponds to a specific IP address. Every computer linked to the Internet must have its own unique IP address identifier. However, since it is difficult for most of us to recall accurately hundreds of integer strings, whereas we can quite easily recall the names of hundreds of companies, organisations, individuals, and universities, IP addresses have been translated into *domain names*, or, more accurately, all domain names have a corresponding IP address. Thus, although Internet connectivity is based on IP addresses, anyone setting up a Web site first decides on the domain name that they want, say *www.mycompany.com*, and then gets this translated into an IP address, through a mechanism know as a *Domain Name Server*, so that it can be uniquely identified in Internet space.

Domain names are read from right to left. The letter strings on the extreme right are known as the *Top Level Domains* (TLDs). For all countries, **except the**

USA, the country code may be the top level domain, as in *www.lse.ac.uk*. These top level domains are *geographical*. Outside the USA, the next string to the left is referred to as a *global* TLD (gTLD). It designates a specific type of activity, rather than a geographical location, as the *gov* in ***http://www.pro.gov.uk***, indicating that this is a government-related site. In the USA, the global TLD is invariably indicated by the TLD, that is, the string on the extreme right, the *gov* in ***http://www.senate.gov***, for example.

Until recently there were seven global TLDs:

com designating a commercial organisation (*www.microsoft.**com***)

net designating a network (*www.demon.**net***)

org designating an international or other organisation (*www.un.**org***)

edu designating a US educational institution (*www.harvard.**edu***)

int designating an organisation established by international treaty (*www.nato.**int***)

mil designating a US military Web site (*www.af.**mil***)

gov designating a government Web site (*www.senate.**gov***)

The first three are open to anyone, being allocated on the basis of commercial terms. The latter four are available only to applicants who meet specific requirements. To use the **edu** gTLD the site must be part of an educational institution offering four-year college courses. The specific requirements for the others are implicit in the designation.

In the UK, the **com** gTLD is frequently replaced by **co**, although you cannot tell whether a company/business is in fact UK based from this. Similarly, educational institutions are designated by **ac** rather than by **edu** in the UK. Also, in the UK, the **gov** TLD is followed by the country code TLD, as in **www.pro.gov.uk**.

Because the Internet is getting rather crowded, and the above list does not offer a sufficiently broad range of different types of activity, additional gTLDs have recently been agreed, some of which have already been introduced:

aero Air Transport Industry (authorised for signature)

biz Businesses (fully operational)

coop Cooperatives (approved and signed)

info Unrestricted use (fully operational)

museum Museums (fully operational)

name Individuals (operational for test purposes)

pro Initially for accountants, lawyers, and physicians, but other professions will follow (under negotiation)

Many URLs also include, after the protocol http://, *www*, as in ***http://www.pro.gov.uk***. This is included to designate the computer on which the resource is located.

To see where we have arrived at, examine the URL

http://clawww.lmu.edu/faculty/lswenson/Learning511/learning.html

This is divided into two main components:

1. *http://clawww.lmu.edu*

2. *faculty/lswenson/Learning511/learning.html*

The first part provides the information that the resource (*learning.html*) is located on a computer (*clawww*) serving up Web pages, located at *lmu* (Bellarmine College of Liberal Arts, Loyola Marymount University, Los Angeles), and that it is an educational institution (*edu*). The second part tells us that the file name of the resource is *learning.html*. It also tells us that it is in a directory called *Learning 511*. This could be useful, as it implies that there might be more than one file relating to *learning* in that directory. *Learning 511* is a sub-directory of the *lswenson* directory, which, in turn, is a sub-directory of the *faculty* directory. This suggests that the resource has been provided by L. Swenson, who is a member of faculty at Loyola Marymount University. It also suggests that one of the modules that is offered there is Learning 511. In short, the URL has provided a lot of information about the location of the file, its authority (educational establishment/member of faculty), and, perhaps, links to other online resources from this source on *learning*.

Assume that at some time you accessed this file, but subsequently, some considerable time later, you find that when you use that address you receive the ubiquitous *page cannot be found* error message. Alternatively, you could have been led to this page by a search engine reference, or a dead link from another site. What could have happened to this file? Regard *permanent deletion* as a worst-case scenario. The most likely solution is that the file has been relocated in yet another one of those Web site restructurings necessitated by lack of forward planning.

A workable approach to this is to move right to left across the URL, deleting blocks between slashes and pressing the return key. So, starting with *http://clawww.lmu.edu/faculty/lswenson/Learning511/learning.html*, lop off *learning.html*, then *Learning511/* until you arrive at the domain name *claawww.lmu.edu*. Somewhere along the route you may find an indication as to where the file has been moved. Perhaps the materials relating to *Learning 511* have been merged with those originally in another directory, or, the *Faculty* directory may have changed, which you could establish from the University Home page, at *http://clawww.lmu.edu*. Also, on university Home pages there invariably is a search engine, or a link to faculties. Given the hypothesis that the author of the file is L. Swenson, key this in, or locate the name from the faculty list, and then hope to locate the file from L. Swenson's Home page.

If none of that worked, and I had not found any reference to L. Swenson on the faculty listing, or in using the search engine, if available, and I was really keen to trace this file, I would assume that L. Swenson might have moved to another institution and transferred his materials there. Using a search engine I would try to locate L. Swenson. As most people are creatures of habit, and as, also, universities are inclined to give staff directories for their Web materials using their initials and names, I would use the AltaVista URL search feature to locate files with directories *lswenson*, using the syntax, *url:*swenson**. Alternatively, if you know the title of the document (text title), or a phrase from it, use this in a search engine. If you were referred to a file from a search engine, use the information provided, which frequently consists of the first few sentences and the title, as the query syntax. Something other than the title may be more useful, because, if the file is linked to from other sites, the title is the most likely attribute to be used for the text link, and you will, therefore, receive many hits that constitute links to the original URL, which you know is not available.

Thus, to locate files, and information on their authors, when this is not readily made available, you have to engage in some sleuthing. The top level domain gives you information on the type of organisation that uploaded the file, which frequently has some bearing on the probability of the file having been deleted; this is more likely in the case of an educational institution or commercial organisation than an international agency such as the UN. The directory structure can indicate what type of resource it is, and who authored it. Information on the referring page can also provide some useful data. If this has a link to a resource that is not available, and the page was last updated five years ago (and there are many of these), it is more likely that the file has been deleted than if the page was updated two months ago, and there is a statement that all the links were last checked six months ago.

Let's go back to where I more or less started, my quest for the author of a chapter dealing with *Pavlovian Conditioning*, the URL being:

http://highered.mcgraw-hill.com/olc/dl/27748/kle90462_ch03.pdf

From the domain name it is clear that the provider of this file is the publisher McGraw-Hill, who obviously had a lot to learn about Web marketing. Having chopped off the file name, I found two files in the 27748 directory, one of which had a file name that ended in *pref.pdf*. An obvious guess is that this could be the Preface, which it was, and which identified the name of the publication and its author. A few keyboard strokes later to the Amazon site, and the publication date was retrieved.

Finally, an example illustrating how a close examination of a URL can assist in rescuing us from another common source of *page cannot be found* files: typographical errors. In an essay with many hyperlinks, *A Rough Chronology of Jean Baudrillard's Thoughts on the World* at ***http://www.genesco.edu~bicket/***

panop/baudrillard.htm, one of the terms hyperlinked is *simulation*, this concept, and *simulacra*, being key Baudrillian concepts. However, the link leads to definitions of terms beginning with P, the URL for which is ***http://www.genesco.edu~bicket/panop/subject_P.htm***. It is quite easy to see that it is highly likely that if you substitute an S for a P in the above, it is probable that you will find the location of the definitions of those terms, which was in fact the case.

3

Evaluating and referencing Internet resources

3.1 Evaluation: introduction

The rate of growth of the Web is phenomenal and is expected to increase at a faster rate as the technology and knowledge of its use spread further geographically and demographically. Developments effecting connectivity to Web servers and the writing of Web pages have made Web publishing substantially easier and within the economic means and technical competency of large numbers of people. Whereas five or six years ago Web publishing was considered a *skilled* activity that required some training, this is no longer the case to the same degree. In addition, many organisations, businesses, and individuals consider that it is imperative to have an online presence. For individuals this has become increasingly easier as *free* Web space is often part of the package that subscribers to Internet Service Providers are automatically offered. Also, many institutions of higher education offer their students and staff Web space and technical assistance.

These and other factors have contributed to the mushrooming of the number of Web sites that are publicly accessible, and to the enormous number of Web pages that have been published. Hundreds of thousands of new ones are added daily. Some of the prerequisites to securing publication in print do not, for the most part, obtain in this medium. There is no need for submission of proposals to publishers and editorial committees with the attendant refereeing processes. Commercial and scholarly considerations operate to a substantially lesser degree, if at all. Finally, there is no post-publication evaluation system in place that approximates reviews published in scholarly journals, bibliographies, and citation indexes.

It is hardly surprising, therefore, that alarm bells have been rung about the quality and reliability of materials that appear on the Web.[1] While there is much good sense in many of the critiques, they also display a degree of naiveté about printed sources of information.[2] Matthew Ciolek, for instance, has noted

> There are no commonly accepted standards for the presentation of online information. Instead, there is an ever-growing proliferation of publication styles, page sizes, layouts and document structures. Moreover, links to other Web resources tend to be established promiscuously, that is without much thought for the target's relevance or quality. There is also a pronounced circularity of links. . . . Finally, emphasis continues to be placed on listing as many hypertext links as possible – as if the reputation and usefulness of a given online resource depends solely on the number of Web resources it quotes. In practice this means that very few such links can be checked and validated on a regular basis.[3]

While many examples can be found on the Web to illustrate the points made, I think that it will be patently obvious to many readers of articles that appear in professional scientific journals and edited collections, as well as monographs, that in a sizeable number of instances the value-added knowledge that is provided in such sources is often equally limited. The 'ever-growing proliferation of publication styles, page sizes, layouts and document structures' certainly characterises printed publications; indeed, many readers consider this a valuable attribute of the medium. There is also a tendency, which is not too difficult to document, to believe that the *authority* and *scholarship* of a work is to be measured in the number of citations and direct quotes that are included in it, despite the fact that that which is referenced is often inherently mundane and non-contentious. Circularity of links is as much evident in the printed as in the online literature, albeit in the former it appears in the form of bibliographies rather than hypertext links.

A prudent conclusion would seem to be that common standards of information evaluation should apply across publication media.[4] At the same time, it is necessary to recognise that these need not be applied with the same degree of stringency in each instance. Thus, it is reasonable to assume that a monograph published by a reputable university publishing house has undergone an established and relatively rigorous review procedure, and that its authority is thereby established. Its quality and accuracy will be subject to a wider review process of which anyone can appraise him- or herself. This does not immediately apply to the majority of Web publications. Thus, although the same criteria may apply, the mode of their establishment will vary.

3.2   Evaluation criteria

The criteria that those accessing information materials are recommended to take cognisance of fall within the realms of common sense rather than rocket science. Before enumerating and annotating some of these, a distinction should be drawn between two types of site, although combinations of the two are very common. I will refer to them as *Links* and *Information* sites.

(1) Link sites

The *Links* site, of which there are a number of sub-types, primarily provides information on other Web sites that deal with particular topics. They include subject gateways, subject directories, and lists of links. They may be annotated hyperlinks, or just a list of titles with hyperlinks. I assess the uses and utility of such sites in Chapter 5. As they do not provide subject content information, considerations of the authority of the compiler or the nature of the organisations publishing the resource are of secondary importance. It is nearly always the case that an annotated list of links will prove more useful and time efficient than a mere list of hyperlinks. The latter, in my opinion, are generally not worth the effort of scrutinising or downloading.

Frequently, the pages linked to are just another set of links. Link sites that are maintained by libraries, or government established or funded organisations, are likely to be more useful than other such sites, if only because they frequently employ dedicated personnel whose job includes researching and annotating online resources. However, there are many personal Web sites that include annotated lists on specialist fields that the higher education librarian does not attend to. What is important as far as annotated link sites are concerned is their comprehensiveness relative to the online resources that are available, their currency, the adequacy of the resource classification criteria employed, the descriptive quality of the annotations, and the site search facilities that are available. Good annotated link sites also provide links to other sites that reference overlapping subject matter.

Some of the points made below in relation to information sites apply also to link sites.

(2) Information sites

There is some overlap between *link* and *information* sites, inasmuch as a good information site will also provide links to other Web resources that provide information and data dealing with the same subject matter, the more useful of these being annotated. Information sites provide data or texts relating to particular subject matters in the form of statistical series, electronic books, image, audio, and video archives, minutes of meetings, international conventions, laws and regulations, news items, primary documents, secondary literature, reference materials, points of view, personal biographies, travel experiences, and so forth.

When authors refer to the problem of evaluating Web sites, what they point to is the difficulty of assessing the intellectual content and provenance of these materials. There is substantial agreement among authors that in evaluating the information available at a site the following should be considered in weighing up the reliability of the information made available:

Authorship Does the page provide information on the author of the document, or the compiler of the page? The two are not necessarily the same, as, for instance, with international conventions, historical documents, maps, and electronic textbooks. Any pages that are not traceable to an author or organisation should be regarded warily; it is invariably advisable to find another source for the same information. It should be taken as a *sine qua non* of standard Web page authorship and compilation that a named individual or organisation should be specified, or that it should be attributable to an organisation by its logo or URL (e.g. *www.un.org*). Authorship, although not explicitly documented on particular pages, is frequently traceable, but this often requires the additional effort of following links provided on the page to the Home page, or moving back along the URL.

Many writers consider that it is important that contact details to the author be provided. My own view is that this is sometimes helpful, as much to the author as to the user, but not necessarily an essential criterion in the evaluation of the materials on a site/page. Some authors may quite deliberately fail to provide these because of the potential attendant increase in the volume of email that they will receive.

Authority of the author What are the qualifications of the author relative to the material that is provided? Although it does not necessarily always follow that material provided by someone with relevant subject-accredited qualifications is thereby useful, reliable, of suitable quality, and current, there is a presumption that they are related. Although not often found, it is helpful if details relating to qualifications, institutional affiliation, and publications are provided.

Authority of the material How does the material compare with the information that you have on the subject, or with information that is provided on the same subject from other sites, or from print sources? Where applicable, you should expect to find appropriate attribution and bibliographies.

Of particular importance is whether the source of the material that is provided is referenced. Many documents that are published on Web sites have been scanned, and then converted to HTML or PDF before being posted. Other files have been copied from other Web sites. Leaving aside the issue of copyright, it is important that the original source of such documents be specified. Thus, if you download documents from a site where it is apparent that they have not been authored by the site maintainers, and there is no source information provided, it is preferable to try to locate the original source as it is impossible to ensure that errors have not occurred in the processes of copying, scanning, editing, and posting.

Authors writing on issues relating to Web site evaluation also stress the importance of examining the depth and breadth of the material. This emphasis is misplaced and probably arises from too superficial an attempt to compare Web and printed materials. If you are reading a monograph on a particular subject, you expect that the author will situate the thesis being advanced in the context of published literature on the subject. Web sites are not bounded volumes. If you are looking for the UN Declaration on Human Rights, or a map of Ethiopia, the fact that on the same site you cannot find the Convention on Torture, or maps of other African countries, is not especially problematic, as these others can usually be found within another 20 seconds on some other site.

Authority of the site/organisation It is a reasonable assumption that material provided on the Web site of a major international organisation, a research institute, a think tank, or a college or a university is likely to be more authoritative than similar material on a personal Web page or site. Thus, materials on the Web sites of the United Nations, the IMF, the World Bank, the International Crisis Group, MIT, the Law Society, the International Sociological Association, the US Supreme Court, and similar are presumed to be authoritative. If the same document is found on a personal Web site as on that of a more authoritative site, and you want to refer to this document as a source in some context, you should reference the more authoritative site.

Elizabeth Kirk, of Johns Hopkins University, makes the valid point, which applies as much to the author as to the organisation on whose server the author publishes, that an assessment should be made as to whether the organisation is recognised in the particular field to which the materials apply.[5]

It is, however, necessary to be cautious, and consider the site in the context of that of the author. Students publish Web pages on university and college sites, and on the sites of many established organisations there are often disclaimers attached to files specifying that the views of the author are not necessarily those of the organisation on whose site the information is published. Also, I have come across many pages/presentations compiled by individuals unattached to *authoritative* organisations that are unrivalled in terms of the breadth and depth of the subject matter they address elsewhere on the Web.

Currency Although not always important, the currency of the material presented may at times be taken as an indication of site management policies. Good Web designers/authors include details that inform users when the pages they are viewing were last updated. This is particularly important in relation to sites that provide materials on current affairs, technical developments, products, and the like. Quite a few sites follow the cycle of vegetative life in deserts following rain: they sprout, burst into wondrous colours for a few days, wither and seed, bursting into life only years later, if at all. However, lack of a date, although mentioned as important by many authors, is often more of an annoyance and an indication of sloppiness than being of material importance.

Pressure groups/objectivity Quite a few authors note that there are many sites on the Web that provide information relevant to particular fields that are uploaded on the sites of advocacy groups.[6] Thus, the anonymous librarian author of *Evaluating Internet Resources*[7] cautions that those accessing files should ask why the author and organisation publishing the material are providing the information: 'Be aware that most people have an agenda. Is the information biased? Is it designed to sway opinion? From whose perspective is it given?'[8]

While this applies equally to publications in print, it is also largely beside the point. It does not follow that such information is to be discounted merely because it is published by an advocacy group, as it may be that the social scientist accessing the information is especially interested in the views of such groups, how they present information related to their objectives, etc. Information sources need to be assessed in the context of the goals of the persons reading and utilising the information. A social scientist accessing a white supremacist organisation such as the *Aryan Nation* will evaluate and use the information differently from members and sympathisers of the Anti-Nazi League, or employees of the Equal Opportunities Commission, Amnesty International, and the police. While the objectives of those making the materials available need to be taken cognisance of, it does not follow that the information is useless merely because it advocates a particular point of view.

The above are, to my mind, the most important criteria that should be considered when assessing the authority and provenance of materials accessible on Web sites. Many others have been mentioned and among those more frequently discussed have been issues connected with Web site/page design. Some of the points that are singled out in this context are somewhat spurious. They include user friendliness, required computing environment, ease of finding the information on the site, and logic of organisation. All these are, of course, important, but content is king. The site may be poorly organised, require software that needs to be downloaded, and include atrocious background graphics that make reading tortuous, but if this is the only source from which the information is available, and if it is worth having despite the cost in time and the frustrations involved, then the other matters are of peripheral significance. If there are other sites that stand up better on these dimensions, then, of course, they are to be preferred.

In the final analysis, Web site authority and reliability are scaleable. At one end of the continuum it is possible to find many documents that are well presented by authorities in the field who are working for established and authoritative organisations, or by well-respected organisations, which provide as a matter of course details relating to the origins of the documents, the author, and the mission of the organisation. Such documents are as *authoritative* as those that are available in the highest quality printed publications, or, if not available in print, they are on a par with them in terms of all the usual scholarly attributes. On such Web files users can generally place high reliance. At the other end of the scale, there are anonymously provided documents that are poorly presented, on sites that are badly organised and designed, and that include the expression of purely personal opinions unadorned with reasoned arguments. Although the latter are sometimes useful as the raw materials for social scientific research, they are otherwise unreliable.

3.3   Referencing Internet materials

There are certain characteristics associated with the way in which digital materials stored on Internet-accessible servers are typically manipulated that have implications for referencing them. Once a book, thesis, journal article, news clip, or similar is published in hardcopy, its contents are regarded as permanent. Invariably it is possible to locate an original, or an exact replica, and examine it in detail. Anyone with access to such resources can, at the very least, state with reasonable confidence that the author made a specific statement at a particular place in the manuscript or document. They can be photocopied and photographed to produce evidence of specified content. Those printed sources that are most widely consulted are available in thousands of copies, each of which is assumed to be an exact replica of all others. There may be disagreements over the meaning attributed to specific content, but ordinarily there is no reason to question the fact that it was so written. If changes are made in subsequent editions, it is not especially complicated to note the differences.

Digital files accessible over the Internet diverge in important respects from this model. Because they are so easy to modify and upload, digital files *cannot be presumed* to have the same short- to medium-term stability that printed materials do, even though some files may never in practice be altered. When it comes to referencing printed materials, the criteria of importance are title, author, publisher, place of publication, and date. These variables are presumed to *bind* or *anchor* content. They cannot do the same for digital materials uploaded on Internet-accessible servers.

Anyone who uses the Internet over an extended period soon establishes that many documents that could previously be downloaded from a specific server/

directory can no longer be located there. There may be various reasons for this. Web presentations are regularly being reorganised and files moved or deleted. Site reorganisation may result in files being moved to a different server on the same domain, a different host, or, less frequently, to a different domain.

In referencing printed materials, the place where the item can be viewed is not included in the referencing criteria, with the exception of archival materials. It is assumed that the book, journal, newspaper, score, etc., can be found in some library somewhere. *Location*, however, is a critical variable in the referencing of files stored on Internet-accessible servers.

The second differentiating referencing criterion that is critical is the *date* when the content of the file that is being referenced was accessed. Even if it retains the same URL, it may have been modified in minor or major particulars. Frequent modification of electronic documents is considered to be a *sine qua non* of competent, *interesting*, and well-managed Web presentations. The cost of modification, in comparison with that of printed materials, is negligible. This allows Web authors to add further information, update relevant sections, correct errors, reorganise the order of presentation, incorporate additional links to resources that have become available subsequent to an earlier modification, change aspects of presentation, etc.

Very few Web authors keep older versions of documents on a server along with modified ones. Frequently there is no information detailing the dates when modifications were carried out, or these are overwritten when subsequent alterations are made. Many HTML editing programs incorporate features that automatically update the date of last modification when they are altered. It is impossible, therefore, to know anything about the temporal provenance of such documents other than the date of their last modification. Consequently, **it is imperative** to reference the date at which the particular content that is being referenced was accessed, as someone accessing the material subsequently may not find the same content, even if all other referencing variables remain valid (author, title, location, etc.). If you are conducting research that relies heavily on Internet materials, or on Internet-related behaviours, **it is recommended** that you save the files that you are documenting to a storage medium. The costs of storage these days are insignificant, whereas retracing some materials can be very costly in time, if they can be found at all. Note, however, that when you save the materials **you need to reference them at the same time**, preferably on the file.

3.4 Resource type referencing

The referencing format varies somewhat with the type of resource being referenced.

(1) Web pages

COMPONENTS: printed materials elements + URL + access date

EXAMPLE: UN newservice. 'World Conference against Racism ends with call to eradicate discrimination.' 10 September 2001. *http://www.un.org/News/dh/latest/page2.html#40*. Accessed 11 September 2001

If the file that you are referencing included information on place and date of publication (e.g. an etext of a published book, or journal article), you would include this along with the other printed material elements.

(2) Files from FTP sites

A large number of files are stored on FTP servers, which are servers that are accessed by using a particular protocol called the File Transfer Protocol. They are used particularly for storing software applications, but many large text files, which may be in varying formats, are also stored on such servers. It is possible to access such files either with a special software application, called an FTP client, or with most contemporary browsers. The address principles are the same, the major difference being that with some files, for example software applications, images, and audio and video files, you may just have a file name. Consequently, most of the details included in the example above under the category *printed materials elements* will be excluded.

COMPONENTS: printed materials elements (if applicable) + URL + access date

EXAMPLE: *ftp.ncsa.uiuc.edu/Business/Certification.pdf*. Accessed 11 September 2001

The *ftp.ncsa.uiuc.edu* is the *Internet Domain Name* of the server, and *Business/Certification.pdf* is the path name to the file. If you wanted to access this file using an FTP client, that is the Internet Domain Name and path you would use. If, however, you wanted to access the file using a Web browser, you would have to precede this with ftp:// to indicate that you were using the File Transfer Protocol to access the file. The URL that you would type in, therefore, would be:

ftp://ftp.ncsa.uiuc.edu/Business/Certification.pdf

If the file you have accessed has a title, author, etc. (including place of publication) you would include this in the printed materials components.

(3) Electronic mail

Although in many instances simply noting that X had said Y in a 'personal communication' will suffice for purposes of reference, in some instances a more detailed formula may be required.

COMPONENTS: Author's name/alias + Subject + Author's email address + Date sent

EXAMPLE: Blair, Tony. *'Shifts to the Right'*. **blair@he.gov.uk**. 12 September 2001

(4) Mailing list messages

The referencing of postings made to mailing lists requires the inclusion of additional variables to those used in referencing electronic mail messages. The email addresses of authors and of the lists to which they were posted are different. The message may subsequently be accessible from list archives and the address of the list should, therefore, be included in the reference. Another complicating factor is that mailing list messages are organised by subject. As the same author may send a number of messages on the same subject on a particular date, it is necessary also to include the time that the message was sent.

COMPONENTS: Author's name/alias + Author's email address + Title (Subject Heading) + Date sent + Time sent + List name + List address

EXAMPLE: Smith, James. (*Jsmith@mit.edu*) *'Cocaine Addiction and Rehabilitation'*. Sent 12 September 2001, 15:37. ADDICT-L. **listserv@kenvm.bitnet**

(5) Newsgroups

The model for referencing newsgroup communications parallels that for mailing lists and should apply equally well to other discussion groups, including those on local area networks. As far as the latter are concerned, you will need to give some indication of where the resource is located, despite the fact that the communications may not be publicly accessible. Newsgroup articles are threaded, which means that all responses to a particular message are part of the same thread. If an author makes more than one of these in a day, then there will be more than one article with the same author name, date, and title. They may, however, be differentiated by having a number on the subject line indicating its place in the sequence of messages. The only way of distinguishing between them effectively is by including the time of the posting as well as the date. The information that should be provided includes the name or alias of the author of the communication, the author's electronic address, the subject of the communication, date and time of the communication, and the name of the newsgroup.

COMPONENTS: Author's name/alias + Author's email address + Title (Subject Heading) + Date sent + Time sent + Newsgroup name

EXAMPLE: hambone (***hambone9@ix.netcom.com***). *'Feminism is not the Story of their Lives: A Book Review by Christinna Hoff Sommers'* (13 July 1996), sent 22:37. *alt.feminism*

Notes

1. See the long list provided by Auer, N. J., Virginia Tech Libraries, in *Bibliography on Evaluating Internet Resources*, updated 14 June 2002, at ***http://www.lib.vt.edu/research/libinst/evalbiblio.html***, accessed 5 September 2001; Smith, A., *Evaluation of Information Sources*, the World Wide Web Virtual Library, updated 14 June 2002, at ***http://www.vuw.ac.nz/~agsmith/evaln/evaln.htm***, accessed 5 September 2001.
2. For the most part I use the terms data and information synonymously in the present context, while appreciating the distinction between them.
3. Ciolek, M., *The Six Quests for The Electronic Grail: Current Approaches to Information Quality in WWW Resources*, 1996. Available at ***http://www.ciolek.com/PAPERS/six-quests1996.html***, accessed 14 June 2002.
4. This is a point made by, among others, Smith, A. G., Testing the surf: criteria of evaluating Internet information resources. *The Public-Access Computer Systems Review*, Vol. 8, No. 3, 1997. Available at ***http://info.lib.uh.edu/pr/v8/n3/smit8n3.html***, accessed 14 June 2002.
5. Kirk, E. E., *Evaluating Information Found on the Internet*, 1996, last modified 6 May 2002, at ***http://www.library.jhu.edu/elp/useit/evaluate/index.html***, accessed 14 June 2002.
6. *Ibid*; Swoyer, C., 'Evaluating Material on the Net', Chapter 6 of *Critical Reasoning: A User's Manual*, at ***http://www.ou.edu/ouphil/faculty/chris/net.html#18***, accessed 14 June 2002.
7. St Norbert College, at ***http://www.snc.edu/library/eval1.htm***, accessed 14 June 2002.
8. *Ibid*, at ***http://www.snc.edu/library/eval8.htm***, accessed 14 June 2002.

Part II

LOCATING INTERNET RESOURCES

4

Indexing the Internet: subject directories, gateways, and search engines

The efficient location of Internet resources requires knowledge of the indexing systems and procedures of search engines, and of subject directories and gateways. Such knowledge is also relevant to deciding which of the thousands of search engines available should be employed for specific purposes.

For a variety of reasons it is impossible to establish at any moment in time how many files could be accessed jointly through a Web browser or FTP client. In October 2000, researchers at the University of California estimated that there were some 550 billion Web-connected documents stored on publicly accessible Internet servers. Since that survey was conducted, the numbers will have increased substantially. According to *NetNames* (***http://www.domainstats.com/***) on 12 September 2001 there were 36,115,230 domain names registered, that is, unique Web addresses of servers. According to *CyberAtlas* (***http://cyberatlas.internet.com/***), the number of users, worldwide, with Internet access in July 2001 was 171.6 million, of which 112.6 million were active, that is, they accessed Web pages during that month. In June 2002, the number of estimated users had increased by one assessor, eMarketer, to 445.9 million, and by another, Computer Industry Almanac, to 533 million.

It probably matters little to most users of the Internet whether the number of publicly accessible Web-connected documents is 550 billion or 850 billion. Given that few of us could afford the time to trawl through a thousand titles of documents in any one online session, locating those that meet specified criteria necessarily requires access to resources that have indexed these documents in some manner.

Unless you know the URL of the document that you require, the only means of locating those that meet particular specifications is by accessing directories of resources that have been classified by someone, or by using search engines that employ automated means of cataloguing Web resources. In order to efficiently locate publicly accessible Internet resources *it is essential* to understand these systems of classification and indexing. As it is estimated that more than 85 per cent of all files that are accessed are done so through the use of search engines, a figure that is likely to increase further, I will devote most of the discussion to issues relating to them.

4.1 Subject directories and gateways

Subject directories and gateways are very similar, differing across the range only in breadth, depth, and the type and degree of expertise of those classifying the resources in their databases. A subject directory provides links to a wide range of resources by subject type, in some instances to all subject areas. The UK-based BUBL (*http://bubl.ac.uk*) directory, for example, spans academic subject resources. SOSIG (the Social Science Internet Gateway, *http://www.sosig.ac.uk*), on the other hand, focuses on those covering only the social sciences.

A gateway, by contrast, provides links to resources spanning a narrower range of resources; for instance, those relating to news or business. The primary difference, therefore, is in the range of resources covered. A secondary difference relates to the depth of coverage of materials in a particular field. Gateways, as they focus on a narrow subject area, tend to provide more in-depth coverage and annotations of resources in that subject area than a general subject directory does. The more established gateways tend to provide more comprehensive descriptions of site contents.

The overwhelming majority of readers will be familiar with the best known and largest subject directory, Yahoo (*http://www.yahoo.com*, or *http://uk.yahoo.com* for the UK- and Ireland-specific site). Yahoo classifies resources under 14 main headings, including *Business and Economy*, *Science*, *Social Science*, *Health*, and *News and Media*. *Law* is classified by Yahoo as a sub-category of *Government*. The annotations, if provided at all, are brief and rarely give any substantial indication of the resources available at the sites/pages to which they are linked.

In order to track down resources that meet specific requirements with a subject directory, you need to decide first under which main heading it is classified, select it, and then select a sub-category that appears on the page that is returned. If the link that you are looking for is not included in that page, you select the most suitable sub-category that you consider the resource would be subsumed under, and delve deeper down the subject tree.

> EXAMPLE: To locate the Home page of the International Court of Justice, an obvious sequence would be through Government and then Law. On the Law page there is a link to *International*, where there is a link to the International Court of Justice. An alternative route is Government/ International Organizations/United Nations/International Court of Justice. Via either route, it was necessary to download a number of pages to locate a link to this site.

Yahoo, like other directories, does have an onsite search engine that will search within the whole of Yahoo, or a particular category. The query *International Court of Justice* did return a link to the site at the top of the returned list. However, the same was achieved by using the search engine Google, which has a database that is larger many times over than that of Yahoo, which permits more sophisticated searches, and which allows searches within searches. Also, the example used for illustrative purposes was a relatively simple one. The more specialised your information requirement, the more time consuming it is to use a general subject directory such as Yahoo, and the more uncertain it is that you will locate the resource/information required. The very limited annotations that are provided by Yahoo hardly justify the added expenditure in time in searching through a small database of indexed pages.

I have to confess a strong bias against general subject directories. For various reasons I think that they are invariably an inefficient means of locating resources. Before detailing these, I should point to an advantage for certain purposes, and/or users. If you are uncertain as to what range of materials is available on Internet servers in a particular subject area, or if you are looking for a topic to research for some purpose, say an essay, project, or dissertation, browsing the directory tree of a sizeable subject directory such as Yahoo could be useful.

Although these are advantages that new users should consider, they are easily outweighed by some disadvantages. Subject directories rely on persons classifying resources into particular subject areas, as do libraries in the case of printed materials. The sheer number of Web pages already published, not to mention the numbers being added daily, make it impossible for the numbers of individuals employed in such work to keep pace with changes to this database. Every day the discrepancy between the number of pages that are accessible and those classified by subject directories grows wider.

Second, unlike search engines, some of which index all non-HTML tag components of Web pages, with the exception of *stop words*,[1] subject directory indexers either classify each Web page under a small number of topic headings, or provide a multitude of links to a topic that are not organised in any systematic way other than alphabetically. A good example of the latter is the Yahoo country background page (*http://dir.yahoo.com/regional/countries/*). These pages link to resources relating to particular countries. Although for each country there are links to many resources, it is extremely difficult to obtain an overall impression, as you might, for instance, from the *CIA World Factbook*, or the *Library of Congress Country Studies* series, both of which collate information for all countries under a series of pre-selected topics. If you typed the name of a country into one of the larger search engines, you would end up with significantly more links than you would find returned by a Yahoo query, but equally non-systematically arranged, in terms of sub-topics.

The heading under which subject directory indexers classify resources is a function of the degree of expertise that they have of the subject matter, which, in many instances, is likely to be quite limited. Classification of pages, therefore, can be construed as being overly subjective. The category under which the indexer places a particular Web page may be very different from that under which a subject expert might place it, or that a user might expect to find it under. Similarly, the category tree of a large subject directory such as Yahoo is necessarily idiosyncratic; it could have been arranged differently. You can, therefore, spend substantial time trying to figure out what heading a particular sub-field that you are interested in is likely to be found in a named subject directory, which might be different from the classification system employed by another directory.

Subject gateways are similar in many respects to subject directories. The main and significant difference is that gateway classifiers focus on annotating and providing links to resources in a narrow subject area. Generally, therefore, those doing the classification and annotating are more familiar with the subject area concerned, and have more time to locate resources in that field, and the gateway is, other things being equal, likely to provide more adequate coverage of resources in that area on the Web. The most useful of these are those that focus on a relatively circumscribed field; for instance, news resources, or those that cover a wider range of topics but benefit from substantial funding. Examples of the latter, in the UK, are SOSIG, the Social Science Internet Gateway, managed from the University of Bristol (*http://www.sosig.ac.uk*), and BUBL (*http://bubl.ac.uk*), both funded by the UK government. The first classifies social science resources; the latter tends to be more of a subject directory than a gateway, but focuses on those resources considered to be particularly useful to the higher education community.

Important subject directories and gateways relating to law will be listed in Chapter 9.

4.2   Search engines and indexing

Web search engines are tools configured to query databases of information on Internet-accessible files. These include, but are not confined to, HTML files (Web pages), images, audio and video files, and software programs. The user queries the search engine database by keying in search terms into text query boxes that are part of the search engine's Web page interface, as in Figure 4.1.

Search for: Search

Figure 4.1

A typical search engine page has one or more text boxes in which the user can key in information that can narrow down the search so that files with the specifications required are included in the top pages of the lists of links returned when the query is submitted.

The information that search engines have stored in their databases originates from two sources. First, it originates from direct inputs by humans who wish to ensure that their files can easily be accessed through search engines as soon as possible after they have been published. This accounts for a tiny, insignificant, and dwindling proportion of the total number of files indexed by the major search engines. Second, search engine databases are populated by the outputs of *robot* programs, usually called *spiders* or *crawlers*, which are automated software applications that download pages from Web sites, index them, and use these as a means of tracking other Web pages by selecting the Web addresses that appear on them, that is, their embedded hyperlinks. A crawler program accesses a page, indexes its contents, and stores separately all the URLs that were linked on that page, some of which will be other pages on the same Web site, and others pointing elsewhere on the Internet. These addresses are subsequently used to download the associated files, which are indexed later, in a similar manner to that of the referring file.

Search engines do not tap the entire Web. For some time experts have been drawing a distinction between a *surface* and a *deep* Web. The company Bright Planet, in a study published in July 2000,[2] attempted to clarify the distinction between the two, and quantify the latter. The term *surface Web* is employed to refer to Web pages that are static, to contrast them with dynamically constructed pages. Surface Web pages have a fixed content that is downloaded in full when you access them. All Home pages lie on the surface Web, although the content of some may vary from day to day. When you access, for

instance, the Home pages of the *Guardian* newspaper, or CNN, (***http://
www.theguardian.co.uk, http://www.cnn.com***) you find a series of hyperlinks
relating to documents primarily dealing with issues published in the print
version of the *Guardian* on the day of access, or items in the news covered by
CNN, also on the date of access.

If you access the *Guardian*, or CNN, in successive weeks, most of the
hyperlinks on the Home page in the second week will point to a different set of
documents from those available on the first. Now, unless the crawlers of search
engines happened to *crawl* those pages on the days that you accessed them, the
documents that were hyperlinked to when you accessed the Home pages will
not be included in its database. You can, however, access files from previous
dates by using the search engines that are provided at these sites.

Web pages that are built dynamically, or are accessed by way of an onsite
database, are said to be stored in the '*deep Web*'. They are pages that are publicly
accessible, but that are not routinely indexed by search engines. Because search
engines have not indexed them, quantitative and qualitative information about
them is still sparse. The company Bright Planet, in a path-breaking study,
sampled the contents of a significant proportion of such sites and drew some
interesting conclusions that are of obvious importance in the context of trying
to locate information on the Web:

- The *deep Web* is **500** times larger than the *surface Web*.

- The content of the data available covered by these deep Web sites was
  distributed widely across subject areas, 'with no category lacking significant
  representation of content . . . [being relevant] to every information need and
  market'.

- Although estimations of quality, including those employed by Bright Planet,
  are fraught with methodological and epistemological difficulties, they argue
  that although 'the quality tests applied . . . are not definitive . . . they point to
  a defensible conclusion that quality is many times greater for the deep Web
  than for surface Web sites'.

- There are grounds for believing that such a conclusion might be defensible.
  Employing databases to produce dynamic pages requires greater technical
  knowledge and financial investment than that generally required to upload a
  Web page on free server space provided by an Internet Service Provider. The
  surface Web includes numerous *personal* Web pages, many of which provide
  details only about the person uploading it. Web pages on a deep Web site
  tend to have uniform standards relating to presentation, authorship, and
  quality control applied to them. Many such sites are associated with
  organisations that pay staff to compile Web pages on a full-time basis.

- The deep Web is growing at a faster rate than the surface Web.

Files that are part of the deep Web do have Web addresses, URLs. Every time you access a Web page it has an associated address that is unique to it. However, search engines generally do not index these pages in the course of accessing sites that construct/upload pages through the mediation of a database. Sometimes such pages are found in the databases of search engines because links to them have been embedded in Web pages that link to them. These generally constitute a small minority of the total publicly accessible pages that are mediated through such databases.

Locating directly pages in the deep Web requires specialist software of the type developed by Bright Planet, which can be purchased from their Web site. This can be downloaded and used for a trial period free of charge. Readers who wish to tap the resources of all sections of the Web are recommended to read the detailed report on the deep Web available from their site, and try out the software.

4.3   Search engine automated indexing of the Web

The efficiency with which a user can track down required information using a particular search engine is a function of a number of variables. These include (1) the breadth of Web space coverage of the database; (2) the way in which its contents have been indexed; (3) how up to date the collection and indexing process is; (4) certain attributes of what is referred to as the *retrieval engine*, which is the computer program that retrieves and orders links to files that match the user's search query; and (5) the response speed of the server to the query. As the perceptible differences between search engines in relation to (5) are negligible, I shall not refer to this further.

Search engines, for the most part, map only the surface Web, and this incompletely. It is widely accepted that one of the most important differences between search engines, from the perspective of the searcher, is the volume of publicly accessible pages/files that they index. InFoPeople Project (*http:// www.infopeople.org/src/guide.html* estimated that on 27 March 2001, the numbers of pages indexed by the search engines specified, in millions of pages, were as follows:

Google	Fast Search	AltaVista	Northern Light	HotBot	Excite
675	575	550	310	500	250

Bright Planet estimated that in July 2000 one billion documents were accessible on the surface Web, a figure that was being added to at the rate of

1.5 million files a day. If we extrapolate this figure to 27 March 2001, the date that the above table applies to, the size of the surface Web would have been 1354 million files. This figure is more than double that of the pages indexed by the Google search engine, and more than five times the number indexed by Excite.

Differences in the proportion of pages that are indexed will necessarily be reflected in the results returned by specific engines in response to the same query. Randolph Hock[3] submitted an identical query to six of the major general search engines in 1999, and found that they returned 52 unique records. However, the search engine that returned the highest number of unique records, 27, accounted for only 52 per cent of the total. To retrieve 100 per cent of the total number of relevant records, five of the search engines need to have been queried, although three of them accounted for 90 per cent. *The practical implication is that a reasonably thorough search requires the user to employ more than one of the major search engines in relation to each query if they want to achieve a reasonable degree of coverage of the resources that are available.*

The volume limitation stems from technical, logistical, and economic constraints. These may dictate the 'depth' of trawling that a robot/crawler program undertakes. One program may index the whole of site x, whereas another will index only to a specified depth, say the Home page and all links to pages at the next level down. Consequently, a particular search engine will not necessarily index even pages that are not dynamically constructed through links to databases. The user has no way of knowing what sites a particular engine surveys, or how deep the indexing process on them is taken. The software may be configured to index differently sites that are considered to be of particular importance from others, so that they are tapped to a greater depth and more frequently. This means that indexing will be *biased* in favour of certain sites, that is, documents stored on their servers are more likely to be returned than those on other servers. *Accordingly, the results obtained for identical queries from different search engines are likely to vary.*

Another reason for differences in results relates to the recency of the indexing process. One of the main advantages of Web pages, in comparison with print, is that they are easily updated. Although search engine robot programs regularly re-index pages already in their databases, for most on a 30-day cycle, because these pages are frequently changed while additional ones are uploaded, databases of the larger search engines are invariably out of date in relation to the majority of sites indexed. Some studies have claimed that listings are actually frequently three or four months out of date. This suggests that using some search engines to track down documents that have just been issued will not be the best means of locating them. It points to the desirability of using different search engines in accordance with the information that the user has to hand relating to dates of publication of sought-after documents. For instance, if you want to track down information on recent news items, search engines are not the best means of doing so; a specialised news search engine, or the search engines provided on news media Web sites, are a far better bet. Recent govern-mental reports, laws, and regulations, as well as those of international and private organisations and non-governmental organisations (NGOs), are best traced through their dedicated sites.

As crawling depends on tracking a Web through pages that have been downloaded, by moving along the embedded URLs, many engines dispropor-tionately index older files, as newer ones are not as frequently cross-referenced as those that have been around for a longer period. As the Bright Planet report notes, 'documents with a larger number of "references" have up to an eightfold improvement of being indexed by a search engine that a document that is new or with few cross-references'. Files that are not linked to other Web pages will not be crawled at all, and will remain outside the main engine database loops. Thus, newer files with few cross-references are relatively invisible to crawlers and likely to be excluded from search engine databases.

After crawler programs have retrieved pages, these are indexed. The program that interrogates the search engine's database and delivers the matching results is referred to as the *retrieval engine*. The results identified and returned are a function of the engine's *retrieval algorithm*, a software program built to meet specifications determined by the program designers. This determines which records match the query and the order in which they should be presented. Thus, although two search engines may index the same pages in identical ways, the files identified in response to a particular query may differ importantly because of the varying specifications of their *retrieval algorithms*. Some of the factors that are employed in ranking files that match the query entered by the user include: frequency of occurrence of the terms, proximity of terms employed in the query to each other in the document, occurrence of term(s) in headings of the document, level of term(s) in the classification hierarchy of the document, and the order in which the user placed the terms in the query.

4.4 Main search engine types

There are five types of search engines that are of especial relevance:

General search engines These include the most established, familiar, and widely used search engines. They index a sizeable, albeit variable, proportion of the Web. Although some Web sites might be indexed more thoroughly than others, there is no particular subject focus. The most widely used and efficient search engines in this category are: AltaVista, Ask Jeeves, Excite, Fast Search, Google, HotBot, and Northern Light.

In selecting which of these to use the important variables are: (a) the proportion of Web files indexed, (b) the ease of query construction relative to query complexity, and (c) the sophistication of the query language that can be employed. Thus, for example, Ask Jeeves and Google both allow for natural-language queries, but Ask Jeeves has a database very much smaller than Google, which has the largest of all, and Ask Jeeves only provides for natural-language queries, whereas Google allows for the use of queries that employ some *Boolean operators*. Consequently, I have never found that there was any advantage in using Ask Jeeves rather than Google for any query I have submitted.

On the other hand, while AltaVista has a significantly smaller database than does Google, and does not support natural-language query construction, it permits extremely sophisticated query constructions employing all Boolean operators, parentheses, and ten *special features* variables. The user who can write such queries is able to narrow down searches very significantly.

Although it is probably more convenient to stick to the same general search engine all the time, there are good reasons for not doing so. As mentioned earlier, to extract links to a high proportion of unique records dealing with a particular topic, it is necessary to employ more than one search engine given the variability in the proportion of and the particular pages indexed.

Metasearch engines These interrogate the databases of a number of general search engines simultaneously. Although using these carries the advantage of tapping a large number of documents, some of which are found in some search engines but not in others, there are a number of disadvantages associated with using them: (1) the number of relevant hits tapped can be substantially larger than with one general search engine; (2) they often restrict query syntax to the lowest common denominator, that is, to a query that can be handled by all the search engines that are interrogated; (3) when there are a large number of documents in the interrogated search engine databases that match the query syntax, only a small proportion of those indexed by a particular engine are returned; (4) as the relevancy rankings of different engines vary, as does the query syntax that they employ, this, coupled with the restriction on the number of pages returned, makes it likely that most users will probably find it much easier and quicker to locate the files that they want by interrogating a major search engine directly.

There are a large number of such search engines. My own view is that users will be better served by employing Google, AltaVista, or one of the other main search engines. For those who wish to employ or explore their use, the two meta-engines listed below are probably among the best as they query some of the major search engine databases, and both allow Boolean searching. There is some overlap between the search engine databases that they query.

- Ixquick, *http://www.ixquick.com/*, includes the first ten hits from the databases queried, combining the results in one list, and excluding duplicates. Each record returned includes details of the search engine database queried, and its ranking in the records retrieved therefrom.

- ProFusion, *http://www.profusion.com/*, aggregates results into one list and provides information on the source search engine databases.

Specialist search engines These are search engines that collate information on particular types of resource, or, in some instances, specific file types. For instance, Search Adobe PDF Online (*http://searchpdf.adobe.com/*) provides links to, and summary information on, PDF files accessible on the Web. This is an extremely useful resource as PDF files are less numerous and tend to be of much higher scholarly quality than HTML files. Similarly, SearchMil.com (*http://www.searchmil.com/*) is a database of information on US military Web files. Some specialist search engines are *virtual* databases in the sense that they do not query their own databases of accumulated documents. Rather, they query those of sites that specialise in the provision of certain types of resource. For example, All Academic: The Guide to Free Academic Resources Online (*http://www.allacademic.com/*) queries articles that are published in freely accessible electronic journals.

Person/address locating search engines These are the equivalent of the telephone or business directory.

Site-specific search engines Many Web sites provides search facilities to enable those accessing them to locate online documents provided at the site. There are hundreds of thousands of on-site search engines. Generally, keyword searching is sufficient to locate documents required, although many permit more sophisticated query construction, the details of which need to be located at the site.

There are many circumstances in which it is far more efficient to locate required information directly from sites at which relevant documents are uploaded, than by way of general search engines. They include the following:

- When you know, or consider it probable, that documents dealing with a specific topic are likely to be published online by a particular organisation, and you have no identifiable document in mind. For instance, if the topic concerns poverty in Third World countries, there is a good chance that the United Nations or the World Bank will publish information that is relevant, on a country, regional, continental, or global basis. Searching directly at these sites, which can easily be located by a keyword search in Google, is likely to be much more useful than searching for *poverty*-related documents with a general search engine, which will return millions of links to files.

  You need to take into consideration the size of the databases of the Web sites of specific organisations that are likely to publish the documents that you are interested in. The World Bank publishes high-quality reports but its database is relatively small. That of the United Nations is vast. Consequently, if you are searching for a United Nations document that you know the title of, or that could relatively easily be identified through keywords or phrases that will help to distinguish it from other documents, it will probably be quicker to use Google unless you are familiar with the use of the UN search engine facilities, the classification of documents system it employs, etc. This applies equally in relation to other very large databases of online documents on the Web: US Federal and State government databases, particularly the former, the EU, the World Health Organisation, and other UN agencies.

■ Information only recently published. As noted earlier, general search engine databases are not updated daily, except in relation to a small number of sites. Consequently, if the document that you are trying to locate has been published only within the last few days, or even months, it is unlikely that you will locate it through one of the general search engines, and it is far more efficient to access the site of the organisation that published it. Online news media are usually useful for this purpose if the documents are likely to be considered worthy of mention in printed media as they frequently link to the documents to which they are referring.

■ When the information has only recently been published, and/or relates to a particular organisation, and is likely to be of interest only to a particular category of user. Thus, to find conferences dealing with a particular subject matter, it is best to use a site that specialises in providing information about conferences (query Google with *academic conferences*), or the site of a major professional organisation relating to the subject matter concerned, such as the British Psychological Society, the American Sociological Association, the Law Society, or the Political Studies Association of the UK.

■ Current news affairs are most efficiently tracked by using one of the major media sites, such as the BBC or CNN, or online newspaper sites. Breaking legal news is likely to be reported by *Law gazette.co.uk* and *Legal Week*, both of which are referenced in Chapter 9.

The next chapter discusses details of query construction.

Notes

1. These are very commonly occurring words, such as the, I, you, and me, that are not indexed by search engine software indexing programs.
2. *The Deep Web: Surfacing Hidden Value.* July 2000. *http://www.brightplanet.com/ deep_content/deepwebwhitepaper.pdf.*
3. Hock, R., *The Extreme Searcher's Guide to Web Search Engines*, Cyberage Books, 2000.

5

Search engines: standard searches

The Web provides access to billions of documents, and millions are being added every day. Users are only interested in, and can only cope with processing, an infinitesimally small proportion of the total, say 20 to 100 documents, at any one time. Frequently you may only be interested in a particular document, or establishing a matter of fact. As a source of information, the Web is going to increase in importance, in both quantitative and qualitative terms. Consequently, knowledge relating to search engines, how to query them efficiently, what their respective merits are, etc., is a long-term investment. Although such knowledge will have to be refined as the Web and engines change, the basics are likely to remain the same. Unless you intend to become an Internet specialist, your approach should be a simple one: in and out – fast. Mastering the Web is all about getting to those documents and facts that you are interested in as quickly as possible, and about locating quality resources in a particular field. Part III deals more with the latter. Here I focus on how to maximise returns using search engines. Although the examples I employ relate to legal themes, they apply across the academic and non-academic spectrum.

Mastering search strategies will take a bit of time, an hour and a half for basic searches, and another hour on top for advanced searches, for absolute beginners. Follow the text while experimenting with slightly different queries. In the longer run, the payback will be reckoned in terms of time spent reading the resources located rather than on locating them. If you add time wasted on inefficient searching techniques over an undergraduate course, or a decade, the figure for regular Internet users will be significant.

The purpose of search engines is to assist in the location of files that include information that you are interested in (e.g. legal realism), or meet more precise criteria (e.g. Kelsen's theory of international law). Not all search engines operate in the same way, or will give identical results in response to the same query. As noted in the previous chapter, some index a much larger proportion of publicly accessible Web pages than others. The indexing systems used to break down the pages also vary, so that even if two search engines index the same pages, an identical query served to both will not necessarily lead to the same returns. They also vary in relation to the complexity of the search queries that you can employ to interrogate their databases. Although all allow for elementary keyword queries (e.g. tort, "ponsonby rule" Devlin), some also permit natural-language queries (e.g. criminal law reform). There are yet others that allow for complex advanced searches, requiring mastery of a search syntax that can narrow down results returned far more precisely than when using single keywords, or natural language. An example of such a query is

> "war crimes" NEAR (genocide OR "crimes against humanity")
> AND NOT (Nuremberg OR {Bosnia OR Croatia})

which you might employ to locate documents discussing the relationship between *war crimes*, *genocide*, and *crimes against humanity*, but not in the context of the *Nuremberg* trials, or the conflicts in the former Yugoslavia that involved *Bosnia* or *Croatia*. This query would also exclude references to these issues relating to the Second World War.

In terms of the objectives sought, I distinguish, for illustrative purposes, between two types of query submitted to search engines: *targeted-browsing* and *targeted-searching*. Targeted-browsing refers to searches that are directed at tracking resources in a particular subject area, for instance, files relating to *legal aid*, or *criminal law*. A *natural-language* query (e.g. *resources for legal research*) or just a keyword, e.g. *tort*, will invariably return a substantial number of hits that meet the specifications of that query. Because the scope of the query is quite broad, the number of matching entries is likely to be very large. The construction of such queries does not generally require much skill, and does not necessitate the mastering of specialised query syntax.

Targeted-searching, on the other hand, refers to queries directed at locating files that meet relatively narrow specifications; for instance, the *Health and Safely at Work etc. Act 1974*, or documents that include references to *constructive dismissal* and *fixed-term contracts*. Targeted-searching is very focused, and is directed at identifying rapidly the documents sought. The distinction between the two types of searching is, admittedly, somewhat imprecise, as, with the exception of queries directed at locating documents with specific titles, some degree of browsing is necessarily involved.

If you query one of the larger search engines, which, like Google and AltaVista, index hundreds or tens of millions of documents, with just one keyword, or a phrase that is in common use, you can expect that the numbers of hits returned will be in the order of tens, to hundreds of thousands, sometimes millions. For example, *employment rights* returned 3,660,000 with Google, and 11,788,131 with AltaVista (17,057 for *"employment rights"*; the double inverted commas ensure that it is treated as a unit by the AltaVista retrieval algorithm, rather than as *employment* or *rights*), on 28 August 2002. No one has the time or intellectual energy to search through such lists. My own rule is that if the information required is not included in the first 20 to 40 hits returned, that particular strategy should be rejected or refined. Ideally, the required information should be included in the first ten hits. Although the engine's retrieval algorithm will order the results returned, the user is not party to the criteria implemented, and that ordering may be radically at variance with the users' preferences, or expectations. If you are unfamiliar with the way in which search engines work, how useful they are relative to other sources of information, which type of search engine you should interrogate for the type of document or information that you are looking for, and how to construct a search query effectively, you will end up spending a lot of time searching for the information that you require, and the documents that you eventually settle for may not be the most useful among those publicly accessible.

5.1 Search engine strategy

Although there are hundreds of thousands of data-searching tools that can be employed to track down Internet resources, there are only a few general search engines that are worth considering using regularly. These are search engines that index a substantial proportion of Web space, that have useful search features enabling users to narrow down substantially the number of links returned, so as to reduce significantly time spent searching, whose databases are being continuously updated, and that keep abreast of a rapidly changing database accumulation and indexing environment.

The two search engines that I particularly recommend currently are Google and AltaVista. Google has emerged in the last few years as one of the most useful search engines. It employs a *natural-language* retrieval algorithm, which makes formulating queries relatively simple, and orders the links returned so that those most likely to be of interest are listed first. AltaVista is a long-established engine. It is distinguished from all others by the sophistication of the queries that can be submitted, in both breadth and depth. Although its database of indexed files may be smaller than that of Google, it is very difficult to be certain that this will make much difference to users whose interest is in high-quality academic or professionally focused resources.

Because of the sophisticated nature of the queries that can be submitted to AltaVista, allowing users to significantly reduce the number of relevant hits returned, and ordering the most relevant at the beginning of the listings, I will illustrate the formulation of both basic and advanced search queries primarily in relation to its query syntax. As will be elaborated on below, advanced searches in AltaVista permit the use of Boolean operators, and *phrase* and *proximity searching*. Many other search engines incorporate some or all of these features. The skills mastered using AltaVista's search syntax are, therefore, transferable to many other search engines. Some incorporate these features in the form of drop-down menus. Others allow for some aspects of the syntax but not others. None provides the same degree of flexibility or allows for the same degree of narrowing down of queries.

Occasionally, very occasionally, I also use Ask Jeeves, ***http://www.ask.co.uk***, which I can commend for some very limited purposes. This search engine employs a natural-language retrieval algorithm and does not have any other features that permit the refining of queries. Although fast, its database is small, and can be used efficiently only for relatively simple queries. If you want to track information on train timetables, cinema features, television schedules, flights, and similar, it can be useful. For the type of resource tracking that most students, practitioners, and academic staff are likely to be interested in, it is less so. Nonetheless, having one of the buttons in your *Links* toolbar point to it might be worth while for some purposes.

5.2   Preparing your browser

If you are able to, add the Google toolbar and the AltaVista link button to your browser, as described in Chapter 12. Having done this, when you want to conduct a search, all you need to do is type the query into the Google query box, or link to the AltaVista page; both are much quicker and more convenient than doing this through *Favorites/Bookmarks* or by typing in the URL.

5.3   Some terminology

Phrase searching – queries that include more than one word that are ordered in terms of adjacency and succession (e.g. *"constructive dismissal"*).

Boolean operators – components of a specialised and easily mastered search syntax language that are extremely efficient in narrowing down results returned by search engines that allow their use (e.g. *"actus reus"* AND NOT *"Hill v Baxter"*), that is, references to *actus reus*, but excluding the *Hill v Baxter* case.

Field searching – searching restricted to specified parts of a document, e.g. title, domain name component of address, host name component of address. For instance, the query (title: "*Law Society*") interrogates for resources that include the phrase *Law Society* in the title. Note that the reference here is to the HTML document title, which often is, but need not be, the same as the text title of the document.

Proximity searching – queries that specify that the records returned should include component parts within a default number, or a specified number of words from each other. For instance, the query ("*retrospective legislation*" NEAR "*criminal conspiracy*"), submitted to AltaVista, searches for resources that include "*retrospective legislation*" and also include a reference to "*criminal conspiracy*" within 10 words either side of "*retrospective legislation*". Instead of NEAR, you could use NOT NEAR to locate those resources that exclude a reference to "*criminal conspiracy*" within ten words either side of the phrase.

5.4   Basic searches with AltaVista

When you first access AltaVista at ***http://uk.altavista.com*** (or ***http://www.altavista.com***) part of the document returned looks like the graphic in Figure 5.1.

The first thing to do is to determine whether you want to search *worldwide* or through resources located on *UK* servers. If you know that the resource that you are searching for is stored on a UK server, say a government report, or on a UK university server, select UK. You should **note**, however, that search engines use top level country domain names (see pp. 9–10) to establish the country location of servers, and that this is not necessarily a very accurate yardstick. Also, although a document may appear to be of particular relevance to UK-based residents, or focus on UK-related issues, it may very well have been uploaded on a server with a different country top level domain. Official UK government departments, as well as public service bureaucracies, tend to be over-preoccupied with secrecy, data protection considerations, and similar, which means that at

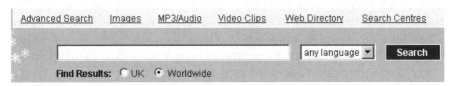

Figure 5.1
Source: Reproduced with the permission of AltaVista Internet Operations Limited.
All rights reserved.

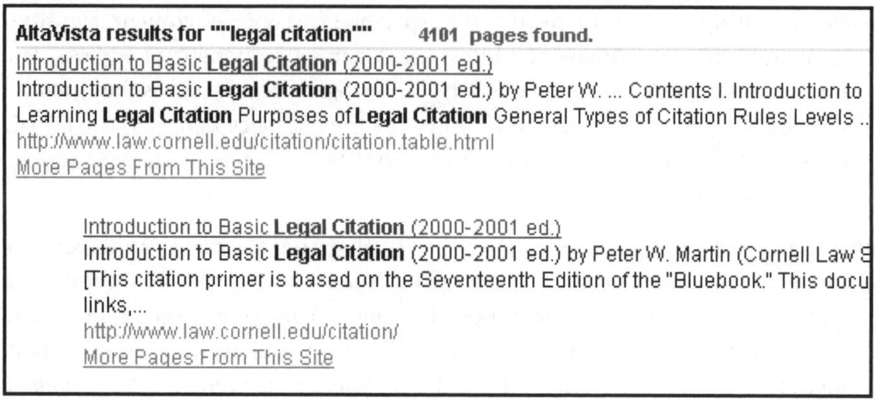

AltaVista results for ""legal citation""   4101 pages found.

Introduction to Basic **Legal Citation** (2000-2001 ed.)
Introduction to Basic **Legal Citation** (2000-2001 ed.) by Peter W. ... Contents I. Introduction to
Learning **Legal Citation** Purposes of **Legal Citation** General Types of Citation Rules Levels ..
http://www.law.cornell.edu/citation/citation.table.html
More Pages From This Site

    Introduction to Basic **Legal Citation** (2000-2001 ed.)
    Introduction to Basic **Legal Citation** (2000-2001 ed.) by Peter W. Martin (Cornell Law S
    [This citation primer is based on the Seventeenth Edition of the "Bluebook." This docu
    links,...
    http://www.law.cornell.edu/citation/
    More Pages From This Site

Figure 5.2
Source: Reproduced with the permission of AltaVista Internet Operations Limited.
All rights reserved.

times you are more likely to find particular documents on US than UK servers. Although using *worldwide* will throw up a lot more hits, if you have composed your query carefully, employing this option should not make a substantial difference.

At the bottom of the AltaVista home page is a list of other AltaVista country-specific search engines. If you consider that the document that you are trying to locate is most likely to be on a German or French server, select accordingly.

The final default that may need to be adjusted is that of the language in which the document is written. The default is *any language*, but you can select from the list provided on the drop-down menu. The difference between *any language* and *English* is small, but large if you choose some other language. Thus, if you are looking for documents on Freud/*Marx* in German, this will reduce the hits returned very substantially (*any language* = 240,398/443,448; German = 40,427/110,215 with the worldwide option, 27 December 2001).

In response to a query the search engine returns a list of entries in its database that link to resources that, in terms of its retrieval algorithm, *match* the query submitted, as illustrated in Figure 5.2, this being the AltaVista response to the query "*legal citation*". In addition to the list of links, the file returned also enumerates the number of entries in its database that match the query; in Figure 5.2 this is 4101. AltaVista and Google both list ten entries per page by default and do not appear to restrict the number of entries that can be followed up.

Conducting keyword basic searches is a relatively simple operation. Decide on your search terms, choose the most appropriate search parameters from those available (Worldwide/UK, Language), and select the Submit button. The query can include characters and numbers.

In constructing basic queries for AltaVista you need to formulate them with the following in mind:

- If you include a string of words in the query, documents will be returned that include one or more of them. The query in Figure 5.3 will return documents that include any combination of these words, that is, those that include all three, any combination of them, and documents that include any one of them. (This applies to Google as well, despite the claims made in its help file.)

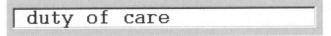

```
duty of care
```

Figure 5.3

- If you want to retrieve entries to resources that include a succession of words in a particular order, they need to be bounded by **double inverted commas**, as in Figure 5.4. This is referred to as *phrase searching*. You would use phrase searching for titles of documents, names of organisations, etc.

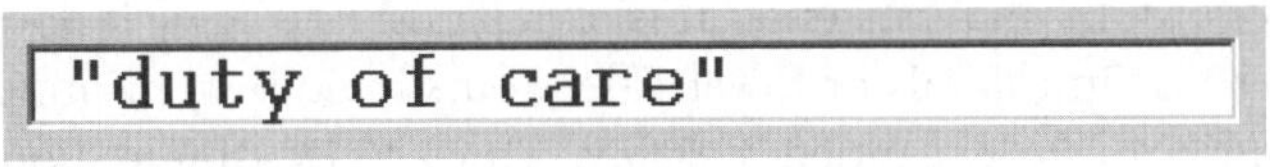

```
"duty of care"
```

Figure 5.4

- To ensure that the entry retrieved *must* include a particular word, it should be preceded with a +. To ensure that a word is excluded, precede it with a –, as illustrated in Figure 5.5. There is no limit on the number of words specified for inclusion or exclusion.

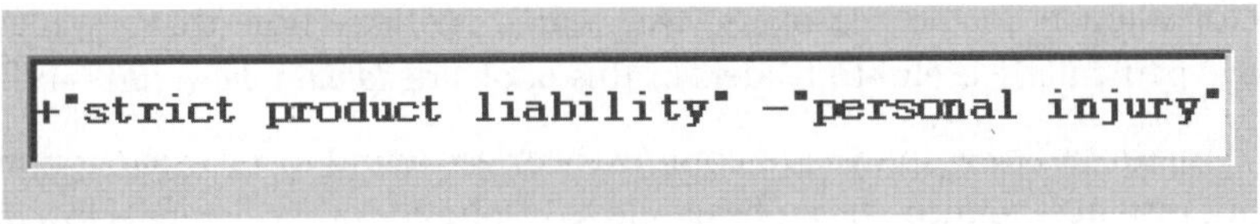

```
+"strict product liability" -"personal injury"
```

Figure 5.5

- Wild cards are used in queries to ensure the retrieval of resources with variable word structures, and are signified in AltaVista by an asterisk. Thus, the query illustrated in Figure 5.6 will retrieve war resources that include various combinations of (war crime, war crimes, war criminals, war

```
+"war crim*" +Kosov*
```

Figure 5.6

criminality, war criminal) with (Kosovo, Kosovar, Kosovars). There are many keyword searches that you are likely to use that can be expanded beyond a basic stem, as with contract/contracts/contractual/contracted. With AltaVista, and most other search engines, but not Google, you can deal with this by using the wild-card parameter, usually an asterisk, but sometimes a question mark. There must be *three* characters *before* the asterisk with AltaVista. The wild card can be used in the middle of the word to substitute for one or more characters, as in "lab*r law".

■ Queries in lower case are capital letter-insensitive in AltaVista. If you type a word in lower case, files will be retrieved that include the word in both upper and lower case. For instance, if you type *pavlov**, files will be returned that include Pavlov, Pavlova, and pavlovian. On the other hand, if you capitalise a query the documents retrieved will only include those in which the word is capitalised. Google is not case sensitive, so that you will retrieve the same entries if you use *Freud** or *freud**.

For many entries that have acronyms, AltaVista and Google appear to return similar results when the acronym rather than the name is entered as the keyword. In AltaVista enter this in capitals; in Google it does not matter whether it is in capitals or lower case. You should bear in mind that many acronyms can be expanded variably. Thus, ICTR (International Criminal Tribunal for Rwanda) is also the acronym for the Ivorian Centre for Technical Research. Check with an acronym dictionary, links to some of which are listed in Chapter 9.

You will frequently improve your results if you employ both the acronym and the expanded version simultaneously.

AltaVista includes a number of special keyword field searches that are very useful adjuncts to the rest of its basic search syntax. Those that are likely to prove particularly useful to readers of this book are *domain, host, link,* and *title.*

■ **domain** can be employed to confine the pages found to a particular domain, for instance, country. It can be employed alongside other elements in a query, as illustrated by Figure 5.7. This query will retrieve documents that include references to solicitor or solicitors, and vacancies, and are confined to URLs that have the top level domain country as *uk*. To illustrate further, you might be interested in locating documents that mention 'legal positivism'. The query ("legal positivism") netted 1434 links; restricting the search to educational institutions, (+*"legal positivism" +domain:edu*), returned 521 (29 August 2002).

```
+solictor* +vacancies +domain:uk
```

Figure 5.7

Generally, you can expect the domain *edu* to return more *academically* relevant documents, than those that do not target a specific domain, for some types of query. Note that the domain *edu*, is a *top level* domain only in the USA, so that the query will locate documents in academic institutions in the US only. You cannot perform a similar search for academic institutions in the UK, as *ac* is not a *top level* domain. The top level domain for URLs of higher education institutions in the UK is uk, as in ***http://www.ox.ac.uk.***

■ **host** will find pages that are stored on a particular computer, as is illustrated in Figure 5.8. This query will find references to *recruitment* on the Law Society server. It can be seen that if you know the host name of the computer, it is relatively easy to find pages that include resources that you are interested in on it.

```
+recruitment +host:www.lawsoc.org.uk
```

Figure 5.8

■ **title** will retrieve links to resources that include specified keywords in the title. By title is meant the HTML title of the page, which may not be the same as the title of the document. This is a very useful feature because a very large number of pages may link to a particular resource, but few, often only one, will have the name of the resource as the title of its Web page. Thus, thousands of pages might include a link to the Law Society, but only Web pages that are produced by the Law Society are likely to include this as part of their title. The query in Figure 5.9 is likely to retrieve pages of the Law Society. Note, however, that *Law Society* may appear in the titles of the Web pages of many law societies, including the Northern Ireland and Liverpool Law Societies. This illustrates why it is very important for compilers of Web pages to attempt to devise titles that tend to exclusivity in relation to titles of the pages of other, often competing, sites.

```
title:"Law Society"
```

Figure 5.9

Pages that include a reference to a keyword or phrase in their titles are likely to focus more centrally on this than those that include references only in the body of the page. Thus, the query *"genocide convention"* returned 3265 hits, whereas (*title:* "*genocide convention*") returned 21 (29 August 2002). Note, however, that the retrieval engine algorithms of most search engines, including Google and AltaVista, will place pages that include the query in the title at the top of the list. Nonetheless, using the *title*: field in the query may substantially reduce the number of pages focusing centrally on the subject matter covered by the query. Of course, there is no guarantee that the quality of the material relating to the query theme included in such pages is superior to those that deal with the same theme, but do not include it in the HTML page title. When searching for specific online texts, it is, this notwithstanding, worth using the *title* field search feature, as in *title*: *"Elements of Natural Law and Politics"*. One other point that you should note is that booksellers also employ key terms that you are likely to use for law searches in their HTML page titles. Thus, if you enter the query (*title*: *jurisprudence*), some of the links returned will be to books sold by companies such as Amazon that include that term in its title. Nonetheless, the number of hits returned will still be markedly less, and more centrally focused on that subject, than if you were to employ the simple query *jurisprudence*.

- **link**. A query using the link parameter queries the database for hypertext links that are embedded in a Web page. This is useful for at least two purposes: (1) tracking Web pages that deal with similar or broader subject matter to that dealt with by the URL in the search query; (2) for site-evaluation purposes.

  Assume, for instance, that you come across or know the site *Electronic Privacy Information Center*, the URL for which is ***http://epic.org/***. If you interrogate the database with the query (*link: **http://epic.org/***), all the pages in the database that include a hyperlink to this URL will be returned. These, it may be presumed, are likely to include a large number that also deal with this subject matter. The number of hits returned might also be taken as *some* indication of how useful or prominent this site is considered to be by those compiling other Web pages. The one caveat is that some of these links will be internal site links, that is, links from some pages on this site, to the page in question.

5.5 Basic searches with Google

Some of the differences between Google and AltaVista are as follows:

- Google employs a natural-language algorithm. So, in theory you should not need, for instance, to include *Elements of Natural Law and Politics* in double inverted commas. In practice, this reduces the number of hits returned. This may not make much difference because the retrieval algorithm places the *phrase* near the top of the list. However, if you are not finding what you want in the first 20 hits, try employing double inverted commas.

- Google automatically treats multiple term queries as + requests, that is, as an instruction to return links to documents that contain *all* the terms submitted.

The order in which the terms are typed will be reflected in the listing returned, although it is not made transparent precisely in what way. If you try this out, however, say with *hart positivism* and then *positivism hart*, you will establish that although the number of documents returned is the same, they are ordered somewhat differently. If you cannot locate what you want within the first few pages of hits returned, reorder the terms and resubmit.

In the help file it is noted that if there is a relatively common word that must be included in the query, precede it with a +, ensuring that there is a blank space before the +.

■ Google treats all letters as lower case.

■ Google does not support *stemming* or *wild-card* searches. So, if you want to retrieve documents that include *contract* and *contracted*, include both terms in the query.

■ Google allows you to filter results successively. Having submitted your query, the results having been returned, scroll down to the bottom of the page, and then select the hyperlink *Search within results*. This will bring up another page with a query text box. Insert the filtering query. You can repeat this as often as you want. Thus, for example, the query *jurisprudence* returned 555,000 hits, reduced to 3540 with *legal positivism*, then to 1180 with *hart*. Note, however, that if you submitted the query *jurisprudence legal positivism hart*, you would obtain *similar* results. However, you may not know in advance how you want to filter your results, basing this on the links returned in response to your original and subsequent queries.

■ For each link that is returned in response to queries, there is a *cached* hyperlink included near the end of the information provided. When you select this, the document that is in Google's cache is returned. This will sometimes be much quicker than waiting for the page referenced by the URL to download. However, it may not be as up to date as the original, which might have been modified subsequent to Google's retrieval of it.

Another advantage to this is that you might be able to retrieve a page that has been deleted from a particular site. If you have bookmarked this, submit the URL as the query to view the cached page.

■ If you have the Google toolbar installed in your browser, there are some additional useful features. Having retrieved a list of hits, selecting the *Highlight* button highlights the terms employed in the query in the pages that are returned. The *Page Rank* feature provides an indication as to how popular a particular link selected from the list of hits returned is. The more green displayed in the button, the more popular the resource. Having selected a particular link, by selecting the *Search Site* button the query is resubmitted to documents included in that site. This is useful for searching large sites, which may include a substantial number of documents that match a query. For information on installing the Google toolbar, see Chapter 12.

5.6 Summary remarks on basic searching

The ability to locate information on the Internet rapidly and accurately is undoubtedly partly a knack, just as is tracking down documents in more traditional archives. A careful selection of words and phrases for your search query will cut down on an excessive number of records returned. It may seem obvious, but if your query does not come up with the results you expected, the first thing to do is to check your spelling/typing accuracy. Remember, also, that in the USA some words are spelt differently than in the UK, and that most Web servers are still located there. It may at times be worth trying both versions. Of course, the differences in spelling can be employed advantageously to exclude US/UK documents as well.

Most search engines do not index single- or double-digit numbers which are not preceded or succeeded by letters, single letters on their own, two-letter words, or some of the more common three-letter words, such as *the* or lower case *and*. There is no point including these, as they will be discarded before the database is accessed with the search string you entered. AltaVista is an exception to this. The search string *my kingdom for a horse* returned exactly the same references in the first ten records as did *kingdom horse*, when using AltaVista. Similarly, the search string *to be or not to be* will not return any useful records in some search engines. If, on the other hand, you included that search string in double inverted commas, a manageable number of matches may be returned.

A few additional pointers:

- Try to think of rare words that are likely to be included in the documents that you are seeking, and unlikely to be found in many others.

- Consider the type of language structure likely to be employed by the authors of the documents that you are interested in consulting (professional academics, lawyers, doctors, scientists, faith healers, politicians, etc.). Try to think of what a particular type of author dealing with a specific subject is likely to include in a document, and then include that in your query, such as leading authorities in the field.

- Include as many words as possible that are likely to appear in the document, placing in double inverted commas those that appear successively.

- Include acronyms and capitalisation where relevant.

Search engines: advanced searches

The information provided in the previous chapter on standard searches should be sufficient for many readers for most purposes. There will, however, be occasions where employing those methods will not readily locate specific documents that are available, or the information that you require. In such circumstances it is possible to substantially improve your locating capabilities by employing some of the advanced searching facilities provided by AltaVista and other search engines. As in the previous chapter, I will illustrate by reference to the AltaVista query syntax, for the reasons detailed there, while also referencing some of Google's advanced searching features. Please refer also to the penultimate paragraph on page 10.

Part of the AltaVista advanced search interface is displayed in Figure 6.1. Your search syntax is entered in the *Query* box. As with standard searches you can select whether the searches are to be confined to the UK, and the language in which the documents are written. If you want to use the advanced searching facilities with other country specific AltaVista databases, insert the country code in the *LOCATION* box. Country codes are provided in a linked file. In addition, you can delimit the time frame/dates. Note, however, that this is somewhat problematic, as, among other reasons, the dates indexed refer to when the page was entered into the database, or those signified in the meta-tags of the document.

The rules for defining words and phrases, and the use of wild cards and capitalisation, are identical with those used in standard searches, as outlined in the preceding chapter.

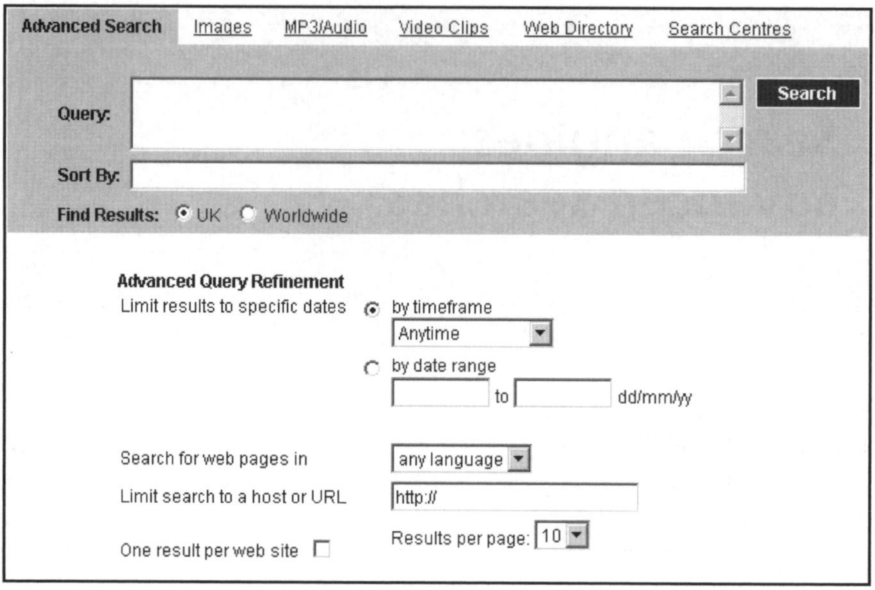

Figure 6.1

Source: **Reproduced with the permission of AltaVista Internet Operations Limited.**

6.1 Logical operators

AltaVista's advanced search features rely on the use of *Boolean operators*, named after the mathematician George Boole, referred to also as *logical operators*. The four operators are *AND, OR, AND NOT,* and *NEAR*. It makes no difference whether they are in lower or upper case, although for clarity it is useful to capitalise the operators. Alternatively, you could employ the symbols &, |, !, and ~. AltaVista also enables the use of parentheses () in order to bind segments of the syntax together in relation to other segments, as will be elaborated below.

The function of AND and AND NOT parallels that of + and – as described earlier in relation to standard searches. If you require that a term or phrase, or syntax segment bounded by parentheses, be included, or excluded, in advanced searches you employ the AND and AND NOT operators respectively.

- The query *"legal citation" AND Bluebook* will select all records with a reference to both *"legal citation"*and *Bluebook*, placing those in which these terms appear in the title, in headers, and in close proximity to each other, at the top of the list.

  This ordering can be overridden by making an entry in the *Sort By*: text box in Figure 6.1. If you entered there the term *Bluebook*, the documents that appear at the top of the list are those that more prominently include the term

Bluebook in terms of the retrieval algorithm. This means of controlling the ranking of documents applies to all advanced syntax query components. Thus, if you have the query (*"legal positivism" AND "critical legal theory"*), you could enter *"legal positivism"* in the *Sort By:* text box, which should result in those documents being displayed at the top of the list being those that feature *"legal positivism"* most prominently.

As noted, the AND operator binds phrases, and also syntax bounded by parentheses, in identical fashion to the binding of single terms. Note, however, that the logical operator *AND* binds less closely than words juxtaposed in a phrase. Thus, the query *"constructive dismissal"* will return files in which the two terms appear proximately in succession. The query (*constructive AND dismissal*) will return all files in which the two terms are located, regardless of how proximate they are to each other in a file. There is no limit to the number of terms, phrases, or units of syntax bounded by parentheses that can be included in any one query.

■ The logical operator *AND NOT* is employed to specifically exclude terms, phrases, or syntax bounded by parentheses from documents returned. Note that *NOT* **must** be preceded by *AND*. The query (*"legal positivism" AND NOT Hart*) will return all files that include a reference to *"legal positivism"* but exclude references to *Hart*. You can employ this operator more than once in a query, as in (*"legal positivism" AND NOT Hart AND NOT Kelsen.*)

Whereas queries that employ the operator *AND* return documents that include all the syntax linked by the operator, *OR* retrieves documents that include *either* of the terms, phrases, or bounded parentheses that are thus linked.

■ The query *"cybercrime" AND ("intellectual property" OR "security")* will retrieve records that include references to *"cybercrime"* and also to either *"intellectual property"* or *"security"*. Observe in this example the function of the parentheses in ordering the components of the syntax. You may employ the operator *OR* to link any number of terms, phrases, or bounded parentheses of syntax. As with the other queries discussed above, you can enter relevant components of the query syntax in the *Sort By:* text box. Thus, using the current example, you might submit that the documents matching the query be ranked by (*"intellectual property" OR "security"*). Alternatively, you could also rank by *"cybercrime"*.

The operator *NEAR* is used to retrieve documents when it is probable that certain concepts or phrases, or a combination of the two, are inserted in a document within ten words or less of each other.

■ The query (*"genocide" NEAR "Nuremberg charter"*) will find documents in which *"genocide"* is within ten words of *"Nuremberg charter"*. The term binds to the left, so that (*"genocide" NEAR "Nuremberg charter"*) retrieves documents in which *"genocide"* is within ten words of *"Nuremberg charter"*, whereas (*"Nuremberg charter" NEAR "genocide"*) will retrieve documents in which *"Nuremberg charter"* is within ten terms of *"genocide"*.

6.2 Parentheses

The above examples of the use of logical operators illustrate that it is possible to create quite complex queries to extract from the database references to records that include sought-after information. As there is no limit on the combination or number of times operators are used in a particular query, working out what the query will extract can become quite confusing. A similar type of confusion can arise in relation to arithmetic or algebraic operations, for instance, $[7y - 15y \div 3 + 5y * 7]$. In the same way as there are rules for ordering operations in arithmetic and algebra, the AltaVista database algorithm orders logical operations in accordance with specified rules.

Alta Vista evaluates the operators that occur in queries in the following order: *NEAR, AND NOT, AND, OR*. This means, for example, that it will perform the search that includes the operator AND before that which includes the operator OR.

Assume that you are interested in tracing documents that include references to the views of either *Hart* or *Kelsen* on *legal validity*. You might construct the query (*Hart OR Kelsen AND "legal validity"*). As AltaVista performs the *AND* prior to the *OR* operation, it will extract all documents in its database that include references to *Kelsen AND "legal validity"*, and then all documents that include a reference to *Hart*, because the query syntax is the equivalent of {*Hart OR (Kelsen AND "legal validity")*}. In other words, the syntax as presented specifies that relevant documents are those that include a reference to *either* Hart, or those that include a reference to *both* Kelsen and "legal validity".

Matters can get even more complicated with more elaborate queries, as with (*Hart OR Kelsen AND "legal validity" AND NOT "Basic Norm"*). Working out the order of operations, and which of the records retrieved ranked highest will include specific components of the information referenced in the query, can be quite difficult. AltaVista recommends, therefore, the use of parentheses when submitting elaborate queries. Operations within them are performed before those outside of them, as in mathematical or algebraic operations.

Thus, reverting to our earlier query, to retrieve documents that include references to *legal validity*, and to *either* Kelsen or Hart, the query {*"legal validity" AND (Hart OR Kelsen)*} could be submitted.

More than one set of parentheses can be employed to bind a part or parts of a query. Assume that we are interested in establishing whether there are any documents that include *findings* or *studies* relating to *problem solving* that reference the theories of *Hart* or *Kelsen*, but *exclude* Kelsen's reference to the *Basic Norm*. The following query demonstrates the use of parentheses in this context:

> *"legal validity" AND ((Hart OR Kelsen) AND NOT "Basic Norm")*

6.3 Google advanced search

Some of the operations that can be conducted by using the *Advanced Search* features of AltaVista can be conducted through the use of drop-down menus accessible from the *Advanced Search* interface of Google, which is illustrated in Figure 6.2.

Although it is possible to replicate thereby some of the features available through AltaVista, it should be apparent that this can only be achieved to a certain degree, and that the features available are considerably less flexible. Moreover, once the use of logical operators and parentheses has been mastered, most readers should find that using AltaVista will be quicker than employing the advanced features available in Google. At the same time, given that the database of Google is substantially larger, I would recommend using AltaVista for complex queries of the type that have been illustrated above, and, if this does not return desired results, use an approximation to the query with Google.

Find results	with **all** of the words		10 results ▼
	with the **exact phrase**		
	with **any** of the words		
	without the words		
Language	Return pages written in		any language ▼
File Format	Only ▼ return results of the file format		any format
Date	Return web pages updated in the		anytime ▼
Occurrences	Return results where my terms occur		anywhere in the page ▼
Domains	Only ▼ return results from the site or domain		e.g. google.com, .org *More i*
SafeSearch	⦿ No filtering ○ Filter using SafeSearch		

Figure 6.2
Source: Reproduced with permission of Google, Inc.

7

Mailing lists

Although the Internet can be thought of as a vast repository of electronically accessible documents, images, and applications, this is not all that it is. While virtually everyone accessing the Internet is interested in using it in some instances as a source of information, there are many who use it as an invaluable medium of interpersonal communication and interaction. Electronic mail is the most visible and widely used instance of this. Two related resources that are used very extensively for such purposes are mailing lists and newsgroups.

Mailing lists and newsgroups focus on thousands of different subjects. There are lists and newsgroups dealing with every major discipline area of the social sciences. Many focus on specialist fields subsumed under them. So numerous are the lists, and so broad the range of topics dealt with by many, that it is at times difficult to establish where specific categories of information are likely to be posted. The same applies to newsgroups, although these are at least arranged in subject-specific hierarchies.

Both mailing lists and newsgroups have much to offer students, teachers, and researchers. This chapter on mailing lists illustrates how to locate lists that meet particular interests, and how to issue basic commands relating to subscribing, unsubscribing, and managing data inflow.

7.1   Introduction

In technical terms, a mailing list is a list of electronic addresses used by a mail exploder (a software application) to forward messages to all those on the list. It refers, thus, to a group of persons who exchange messages via electronic mail on some theme, or themes, that are usually agreed in advance. Mailing lists are an offshoot and development of ordinary electronic mail. The *backend* of a mailing list is a software application that automates the processes of adding and deleting members from the list, sending messages to moderators if the lists are moderated, sending automated responses to queries that are sent via electronic mail to the list by users, etc. There are a number of such software applications. Those most widely used are LISTSERV, Majordomo, Listprocessor, and Mailbase, all of which operate in a similar fashion and provide relatively similar features.

To subscribe to a list, you send an electronic message that includes the appropriate command to the server where the list management application of the mailing list you are interested in is stored. You are then either placed on the list of subscribers, or asked to confirm receipt of a message from the list administration program prior to being placed on the list. Confirmation of your subscription will be accompanied by information about the list, the procedures for unsubscribing, obtaining access to former and future communications, how to temporarily suspend receipt of communications, the format of the messages you receive, and related matters. Usually this is all accomplished in a matter of hours, sometimes in minutes. The exception to this is some moderated lists where the moderator may address further questions to the intending subscriber. Following confirmation that you have been added to the list, you will receive copies of all communications that are posted by anyone to the list. In turn, any message that you send to the list address will be forwarded to all members on the list.

7.2 Locating lists

Before subscribing to a list you will need to locate lists that deal with topics that you have an interest in. There are a number of online resources for locating mailing lists:

- CataList   *http://www.lsoft.com/lists/listref.html*   CataList provides information only on public LISTSERV mailing lists, and only on those in the public domain. Although this may appear somewhat restricted, 242,698 lists were recorded as using this software on 27 August 2002, of which 57,153 were in the public domain. The majority of academic and professional lists use the LISTSERV system, and this listing is, in my opinion, the best one to use, and its lists the most useful to join. The search engine available can access lists by name or title. It also enables retrieval of the names of lists that maintain Web-based archives. Generally, the information available is comprehensive, mostly accurate, and returned speedily. It includes information on how to subscribe to particular lists. In parentheses next to each entry in the list returned are the current numbers of subscribers. Another useful feature is the hyperlink to archives of those lists that maintain them on the Web. If you are in search of academic lists arranged by subject, selecting the title option in the CataList search engine is probably one of the most efficient means of speedily locating appropriate lists.

Not all of these lists are interactive. Some are set up for the purposes of providing information, such as appointments vacant, and the contents of particular journals. There were 513 law-related lists recorded on 28 August 2002.

You can also view lists by host site, by host country, and by the numbers of subscribers. This latter facility is arranged in two categories, lists with more than 1000 subscribers and those with more than 10,000. The information provided is always up to date as it is generated automatically from the databases maintained by the lists. This information can be useful for various research purposes.

- **Publicly Accessible Mailing Lists (PAML)** *http://paml.net/default.html* Compiled by Stephanie da Silva, this listing claims to be the most accurate, if not the largest. The list can be searched by name of the list, by subject, or using the search engine. When you select one from the list that is downloaded, you are provided with basic information, that is, the purpose of the list, the address of the list, and instructions on how to join the list. You can identify the type of mailing list program being used from the contact address, as in *LISTSERV@MAELSTROM.STJOHNS.EDU*, which in this example is LISTSERV.

- **JISCmail** *http://www.jiscmail.ac.uk/* (National Academic Mailing List Service). This mailing list service is funded by the UK government funded Joint Information Systems Committee. The lists are arranged by main subject areas (Humanities, Social Sciences, etc.), which are further sub-divided, and alphabetically. There were 43 law-related lists recorded on 28 August 2002. The service has an extensive Web-based interface, which provides information on joining the lists, and related matters. You can also search the archives of mail sent previously to the list. This is worth doing as many of these lists are relatively inactive and there is little point in joining a list for purposes of exchanging communications with others if these are generally not forthcoming. Unfortunately this service has ceased providing any information about the number of lists, or the numbers of subscribers to them, as was done by the service it has superseded.

Another means of finding lists of mailing lists in particular areas is to submit a query in the form of *'subject' mailing lists* to Google, as in *law mailing lists*.

7.3 Basic mailing list commands and settings

The commands that need to be transmitted in mail messages to implement particular features vary in some details depending on the software application applicable, JISCmail, LISTSERV, or Majordomo. I will be focusing on LISTSERV commands as the overwhelming majority of scholarly and professional lists use this mailing list management package. I will also provide some information on comparable Majordomo and JISCmail commands at the end of each section.

(1) Subscribing and unsubscribing

In order to subscribe to a list you need to send a command to the computer from which the list is managed, instructing the software package to add your name to its subscribers. It is *essential* to send the request to the *administrative address* rather than to the address you would use if you wanted all members on the list to see your communication, the list address. The administrative address is the *mailpackage-name@list address*. For the list BANKLAW-L (the Banking Law list), this is

LISTSERV@LISTS.CUA.EDU

which can be typed in either lower or upper case. To subscribe to this list you place the above address in the *To*: text box of your mail message, and in the body include the message *subscribe "listname"*, as in

SUBSCRIBE BANKLAW-L

which also may be typed in either lower or upper case. You do not need to place anything in the *Subject*: text box of the message. All commands, including subscribing and unsubscribing, are sent to the administrative address of the list. The *unsubscribe* command that is placed in the body of the message, which is sent to the *administrative* address, is *unsubscribe "listname"*, as in

UNSUBSCRIBE BANKLAW-L

There is no need to place anything in the *Subject*: text box.

If you want to send a message that will be seen by subscribers of the BANKLAW-L list, the address would be *listname@listaddress*, as in

BANKLAW-L@LISTS.CUA.EDU

It is very important to get these things right, as some subscribers to lists get somewhat annoyed when those who wish to unsubscribe keep sending the unsubscribe message to the list, rather than to the administrative address of the list. Also, large numbers remain as subscribers to lists because they do not know, or cannot immediately recall, the appropriate command for unsubscribing.

It is important to recognise that the database of subscribers to a mailing list uses the email address of the subscriber, which is included in the header information sent with the email, which users do not necessarily see, to respond to requests, including unsubscribe requests. If you change your email address, obviously you will not be sent communications from the list unless you resubscribe from your new email address. Moreover, before changing to a new email address you should unsubscribe from the list.

If problems arise in relation to subscribing or unsubscribing, you should send an email to *postmaster@listaddress*, as in

POSTMASTER@LISTS.CUA.EDU

Sometimes the email addresses of institutions are changed, the mail being redirected internally to the new addresses. Your communications from the list will continue to be received, but you will be unable to obtain any response to administrative commands, such as *unsubscribe*, because the email messages that you send now include the new email address in the header of the message, which is not included in the database of the mailing list software package. The only thing that you can do in these circumstances is send an email to the postmaster, requesting that you be unsubscribed at the old address, and subscribed at the new one. If you don't unsubscribe from the old address, while resubscribing from the new one, you will receive two copies of each communication sent to the list.

JISCmail Commands:
To: *jiscmail.ac.uk*
Subscribe: *join LISTNAME firstname lastname* (in body of message)
Confirm Subscription: *OK* (in body of message, in reply to message sent to you)
Unsubscribe: *leave LISTNAME*
Unsubscribe all JISCmail Lists: *leave** (in body of message)

Majordomo Commands:
To: *Majordomo@computer address*
Subscribe: *subscribe listname* (in body of message)
Unsubscribe: *unsubscribe listname* (in body of message)

For some lists the procedure may be different. A substantial number of lists are closed, that is, not publicly available, or available to only those who meet specified criteria. Others, although public, are moderated. With moderated lists there may be some delay before the application is scrutinised and responded to by the list manager or owner. You will, however, also be sent detailed instructions about administrative matters relating to these lists.

(2) List information

Lists of mailing list subscribers are useful sampling frames, and their subscribers potentially useful research contacts or subjects. To obtain general information about a LISTSERV list, you use the REVIEW command, typing in the body of the message *REVIEW listname*, as in

> *REVIEW BANKLAW-L*

sending this to *LISTSERV@list address*. Remember that *all* commands are *always* sent to the administrative address. You generally have to be subscribed to the list before you can obtain this information.

The information sent in response is divided into two sections. The first, known as the control section, relates to the list itself. It provides details on the subject matter that the list deals with, who is the moderator/list owner, who can join the list, whether it is divided into topics, and whether it is archived, that is, whether all messages sent are kept in a database. The second section, the subscription part, contains a list of all the subscribers to the list, including their names and email addresses, *except* for those who have specifically requested that this information be withheld, as detailed further below. On some lists membership may be automatically hidden.

You can obtain information just on members of the list, by sending the command *REVIEW listname BY NAME* in the body of the message, as in

> *REVIEW BANKLAW-L BY NAME*

Subscribers will be listed alphabetically using this command, whereas using the earlier command, excluding BY NAME, lists subscribers by host, that is, alphabetically by the domain address of their Internet Service Provider or organisations.

A list of subscribers arranged by country will be returned in response to the command *REVIEW listname BY COUNTRY*, as in

> *REVIEW BANKLAW-L BY COUNTRY*

Note, however, that all those listed under the heading *US* are not necessarily resident there. If the Internet Service or Access Provider of the subscriber is registered in the USA, they will appear on the list in the *US* section, even though they may be resident outside the USA.

Many subscribers to lists are not aware of the fact that their email addresses can easily be obtained by others through use of the REVIEW command. It is not difficult to subscribe to a list, obtain an email listing, and then unsubscribe. To prevent disclosure of your email address through a list that you are subscribed to, send the command *SET listname CONCEAL*, as in

> *SET BANKLAW-L CONCEAL*

If subsequently you wish to have your name reinstated on the publicly accessible list of subscribers, send the command *SET listname NOCONCEAL*, as in

SET BANKLAW-L NOCONCEAL

The information returned with the *REVIEW* command relating to the number of subscribers includes details on the number of concealed subscribers, although not their addresses.

LISTSERV packages compile statistical information relating to lists. The information provided includes details on the names, addresses, and number of messages sent by each member to the list. The command required to obtain this data is *STATS listname*, as in

STATS BANKLAW-L

Summary LISTSERV: obtaining and regulating list information

REVIEW <listname> = *Send me information about the list.*

REVIEW <listname> BY NAME = Send a list of subscribers in alphabetical order.
REVIEW <listname> NOHEADER = Send a list of subscribers arranged by host computer.
REVIEW <listname> BY COUNTRY = Send a list of subscribers arranged by country.
SET <listname> CONCEAL = Do not reveal my address on the list of subscribers.
SET <listname> NOCONCEAL = Reveal my address on the list of subscribers/ default.
STATS <listname> = Send me the available statistical information on the list.

JISCmail Commands:
List Information: *review LISTNAME*

Majordomo Commands:
List Information: *info listname*
Subscribers to the List: *who listname*

(3) Regulating mail flow

Some lists give rise to a substantial volume of daily messages during most of the year. By default, you will receive messages on a per-sender basis, as the mail server receives and distributes them. For high-volume lists this means that throughout the course of the day there will be inputs to your mailbox from such lists.

If you want to reduce the volume of messages received in your inbox you could arrange to have your messages delivered in the form of a digest. Instead of receiving individual messages, you will receive periodically, usually daily or weekly, one message that includes all mailings sent to the list since the last digest was despatched. The length of the periodic interval varies with the extent of activity on particular lists. This option has the advantage of not cluttering up your mailbox with a large number of messages, and allows you to file away digests for future reference if you do not have time to deal with them immediately.

The disadvantage is that it reduces the flexibility of control. When you receive individual messages, you can frequently establish from the subject heading alone what to do with the message. If it is on a topic that you are not interested in, you can easily delete it. If it covers a topic that you are interested in but have no time to absorb upon receipt, you can save it to disk or print for later reading. When you receive messages in digest form you may have to scroll down a very lengthy document, identifying messages of interest. When you do encounter messages that are of interest, you have to decide what to do with them. To print or save them to disk you would have to block them, copy them to the clipboard, paste them into some other application, and then print or save them. It is unlikely that you will want to archive the digest, as it will contain many messages that are unlikely to be of any future interest.

On the other hand, if you are interested in the range of topics that a list deals with, this might be a good option. Digests are probably particularly useful for those on which the volume of messages is relatively small. To receive messages in digest form, you send the command *SET DIGEST listname* in the body of the message to the administrative address, as in

SET DIG BANKLAW-L

There is no need to include anything in the *Subject:* line. If you subsequently decide to revert to receiving individual messages, the command that needs to be included in the body of the message is *SET MAIL listname*, as in

SET MAIL BANKLAW-L

On high-volume lists extended absences can be a problem. To suspend mail while continuing to remain subscribed to the list, send the command *SET NOMail listname*, as in

SET NOMail BANKLAW-L

To resume normal mail deliveries, send the command *SET MAIL listname*, as in

SET MAIL BANKLAW-L

Summary: regulating mail

SET DIGEST <listname> = Mail forwarded in digest format

SET INDEX <listname> = Index of mail forwarded
SET NOMAIL <listname> = No mail until further notice
SET MAIL <listname> = Send me mail on a per sender message basis

The DIGEST and INDEX commands supersede and cancel out the MAIL command. Both DIGEST and INDEX commands supersede each other and cancel the MAIL command. NOMAIL cancels all other commands. MAIL supersedes and cancels all other commands.

JISCmail Commands:
Suspend Mail: *set LISTNAME nomail*
Suspend Mail all Lists: *set * nomail*
Resume Mail from a List: *set LISTNAME mail*
Resume Mail all Lists: *set * mail*
Receive Digest: *set LISTNAME digest*
Suspend Digest: *set LISTNAME nodigest*

Majordomo Commands:
Suspend Mail: *suspend listname*
Resume Mail: *resume listname*
Digests: This can vary between servers, so check the help file for the list.

(4) Help files

There are many other settings for mailing lists that subscribers can configure. For instance, archives of messages, when available, can be searched and messages meeting particular specifications downloaded. Mastering the use of archives can be quite complicated, requiring a reading of the help files, and some experimentation. Archives, however, can be useful for many research purposes, as well as for tracking down information on particular issues.

For information on this and other mailing list commands and configuration settings, consult the help files, obtained by sending the command *help* in the body of the message to the administrative address of the list, for all mailing list packages. Another way of obtaining information is through the use of a search engine, using the query *package-name commands*, as in *majordomo commands*.

Part III

LAW INTERNET RESOURCES

8

Introduction to law
Internet resources

There are a number of different online means of obtaining access to materials dealing with any subject area: through a general subject directory, by way of a specialist subject directory/gateway, through embedded links on a document that you have downloaded, and by interrogating a search engine database. The latter, search engine databases, come in varying formats, from those that index the Web more or less indiscriminately to those that target particular subject areas. These methods, singly or combined, for reasons advanced earlier, and others, will not net all resources relevant to a particular discipline. Moreover, as every reader is aware, discipline boundaries are porous at best.

How you use these various means of obtaining access to discipline resources depends on four things: the type of resource that is sought; the degree of familiarity with the main subject directories/gateways relating to the discipline; awareness of what types of resource are generally available on the Web; and familiarity with search engine characteristics and querying syntax. A user's accessing profile will vary with both professional and Web use experience. Undergraduates, postgraduates, academic teachers, and researchers have different requirements, and will mix access methods variably.

Querying the larger general search engines does indicate that there are a substantial number of *law-related* resources available, mostly free, online. Google returned 48,500,000 hits in response to *law*, 2,860,000 to *commercial law*, and 1,110,000 to *legal ethics*. With AltaVista the figures were 23,969,202, 100,938, and 107,267. (Searches conducted 27 August 2002, AltaVista with the parameters worldwide/English, and employing phrase searching for the last two queries.)

The usefulness of this *basket* of resources will vary by category of user. A very significant proportion will be found to be of little use to anyone. The Web includes an enormous volume of resources that are automatically indexed by search engines, which include discipline/topic-identifying terms (law, environmental law, tort, etc.) that are likely to be of interest to few, if any, other than the persons uploading them. Unfortunately, this includes a large number of academics and aspiring non-professional specialists. Some of these resources are probably uploaded because their authors are simply unaware of the possibility of making resources accessible just on their own Intranets, rather than advertising them to the world. Others are uploaded in the hope, invariably misplaced, of some form of marketing return.

There are, for instance, a very significant number of academic staff, of which there are millions worldwide, who upload *lecture notes* and *slide presentations*. With very few exceptions these are so schematic that no one, except those students who have taken the course provided by the person uploading the materials, is likely to derive any benefit from their perusal. My own estimate, based on thousands of hours of resource hunting, is that in many discipline areas at present, less than 10 per cent of resources will be of use to undergraduate students, and less than 1 per cent to academic staff.

Those who compile discipline- and sub-discipline-related resource directories save us all, potentially, a lot of time and effort, not forgetting those who compile the resources that we are actually interested in. For those who are not as yet familiar with the range of Web resource types available in a particular discipline area, these general directories and gateways are essential. The best list the main resource categories that most users, at one time or another, will find useful.

In the Law Subject Directory I have endeavoured to list resources that I consider are likely to be found useful by persons interested in this discipline. Only those resources that are available without charge are listed, although in the context of annotating these I occasionally point to resources that are available on subscription from the same site. From my comments above, and from the contents of earlier chapters, the reader will already be aware that any attempt at exhaustiveness in this regard is not achievable. By the time I have completed typing this sentence, another five law-related resources will have been uploaded. In compiling this list I have endeavoured to include only those resources that are likely to remain online and kept up to date, where applicable. I generally omit resources that do not comply with minimal standards of authoritativeness, that is, those where it is impossible to establish who the author or uploading institution is, or where the content does not meet minimal standards of intellectual quality. This is not always easy, as sometimes parts of the presentation are very satisfactory, whereas it appears that in relation to other sections, energies have sapped away. Where particularly applicable, I have also omitted those that are not dated.

There are other types of *law-related* resources uploaded on Web sites that I have omitted. If you consult some of the main law subject directories listed in the next chapter, you will find that they include a section called *Legal Areas*, *Special Legal Subjects*, or the equivalent. This will lead to a lengthy list covering specific subject areas: commercial law, criminal law, insurance law, etc. When you select these, you will, in turn, download an impressively lengthy list of links. However, most of these provide snippets of information relating to the topic area, and, for the most part, will not be found particularly useful by most users. Many such links lead to the Web sites of firms of solicitors or the chambers of barristers, where a few choice cases are reported on, perhaps with some commentary and a few additional documents that highlight the authority of the lawyer/firm in that field. However, the selection is invariably idiosyncratic and some of the materials can be found on more authoritative sites. You are not going, however, to find *Archbold: Criminal Pleading, Evidence and Practice 2002*, or anything remotely its equivalent at this stage of Internet development.

I also refrain from listing sites that can only be regarded as *good ideas that may be delivered at some unknown dates in the future*. The *Social Science Information Gateway*, a major UK subject directory, gives a very favourable review to the *Cornell Law Library Legal Research Encyclopedia*, which describes its services as 'a topical and jurisdictional arrangement of all available formats, including print, microform, CD-ROM, WESTLAW, LEXIS and the Internet. Citation to research tools and direct links are provided.' However, at present it is under development, and may suffer the fate of many other Web-promised developments that do not materialise.

There is no magic bullet currently available, and, in my opinion, there never will be one, that is likely to *solve* the problem of locating quality resources. The key is familiarity: familiarity with what is currently available in a particular field in terms of the type of resource, familiarity with the substantive contents that have been uploaded, familiarity with what has recently been added, and, above all else, familiarity with the use of search engines. Browsing through the entries in the subject directory that follows, and returning periodically to the subject directories/gateways for information on additions, will provide a cognitive map of the territory and its changing contours. To keep up to date with ongoing resources in a particular topic, it is necessary to locate those resources that are maintained diligently, and revisit periodically.

9

Law subject directory

*The numbers in brackets after the URLs correspond to the numbered links on the Law Subject Directory page at **http://www.booksites.net/stein**, as outlined on p. xi.*

9.1   Associations/institutes

American Bar Association

http://www.abanet.org/ (1)

Association of Law Teachers (UK)

http://www.lawteacher.ac.uk/ (2)

News, bulletins, notification of conferences.

Bar associations

http://www.hg.org/bar.html (3)

Arranged regionally, provided by Heiros Gamos.

General Bar Council

http://www.barcouncil.org.uk/ (4)

This is the site of the representative and regulatory body of barristers in England and Wales. There is quite extensive information here about the Bar Council, barristers (including their history), the Inns of Court and their work, on instructing a barrister, and qualifications and training.

Institute of Legal Executives

http://www.ilex.org.uk/ (5)

International Association of Judges

http://www.richtervereinigung.at/international/irv/iaj2a.htm (6)

Law Society (*England and Wales*)

http://www.lawsoc.org.uk/ (7)

Law Society of Scotland

http://www.lawscot.org.uk/ (8)

North America – Bar Associations

http://www.hg.org/northam-bar.html (9)

9.2   Case law/legislation

See also 9.4 Courts and tribunals, 9.6 Legal research, and 9.16 Subject areas.

American Law Sources On-Line

http://www.lawsource.com/also/ (10)

Freely accessible online sources of law for the US and Canada. Includes sections on law, commentary, and practice, at the federal and sub-national levels.

Australasian Legal Information Institute

http://www.austlii.edu.au/ (11)

Case law and legislation of the Commonwealth, its constituent territories, and New Zealand.

British and Irish Legal Information Institute

http://www.bailii.org/ (12)

Provides access to freely available British and Irish primary legal materials. As of September 2002, access was available to 19 databases covering five jurisdictions. The courts whose decisions are covered and the temporal depth are too variable to permit listing here. For illustrative purposes, England and Wales: Court of Appeal (Civil and Criminal Divisions) 1996–, High Court (Family Division) 2001–, High Court (Queens Bench Division), 1997–. Materials available relating to Ireland include Supreme Court Decisions 1999– and High Court Decisions 1996–, as well as Irish Statutes 1922– and Irish Statutory Instruments 1922– 1988.

Also available from this source are Scottish Court of Sessions and High Court of Justiciary Decisions 1998–, Sheriff Court Decisions 1997–, Privy Council Decisions 1996–, House of Lords Decisions 1996–, and UK Statutes 1988–.

CLEA (*Collection of Laws for Electronic Access*)

http://clea.wipo.int/clea/lpext.dll?f=templates&fn=main-h.htm&2.0 (13)

Provided by WIPO (World Intellectual Property Organization), a database of intellectual property laws arranged by country. From the left-hand frame select the folder *Full Legislative Texts*, then the folder for the language (English, French, Spanish), and then the folder (not the hyperlink) for the country. This lists the intellectual property acts in the database for that particular country, from which you can select to download the full text.

Court Service (*England and Wales*)

http://www.courtservice.gov.uk/judgments/judg_home.htm (14)

The judgments available from this database, restricted to 200, are selected by the judges concerned, and were handed down in the higher courts, both civil and criminal.

Daily Law Notes

http://www.lawreports.co.uk/indexdln.htm (15)

Free service from the Royal Courts of Justice and the European Court of Justice that provides the most significant updates from the House of Lords, Privy Council, the Court of Appeal, and all divisions of the High Court: 'The cases reported have been summarised and are not the full text version that will appear in due course in The Weekly Law Reports, The Law Reports or The Industrial Cases Reports. What you will find here, however, is a precise and, above all, accurate summary of those cases deemed by our reporters and editorial team to be worthy of a fuller treatment and inclusion in The Weekly Law Reports.' The reports can be searched by most recent cases, by date, by court, and by keyword. There are links to the full reports, which are available on a subscription basis.

EUR-Lex

http://europa.eu.int/eur-lex/en/index.html (16)

This is the European Union portal for EU Law. The site provides access to the *Official Journal*, treaties, legislation, and legislation in preparation, case law, parliamentary questions, and documents of public interest. You will probably also need to access the *Glossary*, available from the left hand frame.

Federal Case Law

http://www.washlaw.edu/searchlaw.html#Federal%20Caselaw (17)

Provided by Washburn Law School. The site provides access to case law of the US Supreme Court, Circuit Courts, US Court of Appeals, federal administrative and executive law, federal statutes (US Tax Code, US Code, Public Laws, Statutes-At-Large), and to state case law.

Finding Foreign Law Online When Going Global

http://www.lib.uchicago.edu/~llou/global.html (18)

Includes sections on sources for finding citations to foreign law, that is, non-US law, full text databases of foreign laws, full texts of international law, and foreign law in English translation on the Internet. This page was compiled in October 1999, but some links may still be found to be useful.

Global Banking Law Database

http://www.gbld.org/ (19)

A database provided by the IMF and World Bank of the banking laws of 39 country jurisdictions, which are accessible in Word and PDF formats. When you click on a jurisdiction for the first time you have to respond to a two-question survey before the file downloads, which does not occur when you access other files subsequently.

House of Lords: Judicial Work and Judgments

http://www.publications.parliament.uk/pa/ld/ldjudinf.htm (20)

In addition to access to the full text of all opinions delivered since 14 November 1996, there is a listing of the current Lords of Appeal in Ordinary and other Lords of Appeal, information on the judicial work of the House of Lords, the Civil Practice Directions, and Appeal Committee Reports.

Interights

http://www.interights.org/ (21)

An international human rights law centre that provides databases of case law, Commonwealth and international, on human rights decisions. The international database can be filtered by subject, state, treaty, and organ, and that of Commonwealth case law by country.

Tribunals

See 9.4 Courts and tribunals.

WorldLII: Case Law Databases

http://www.worldlii.org/cgi-bin/browse.pl?type=cases (22)

Provided by the World Legal Information Institute (*http://www.worldlii.org/*) (23), a listing of freely available databases arranged by court and country.

9.3 Courses/departments/education

See also 9.10 Positions.

Bar Admission Requirements

http://www.abanet.org/legaled/publications/compguide/compguide.html (24)

The American Bar Association's online edition of their comprehensive guide to admission requirements, available in PDF format.

Bar (England and Wales) Education and Training Website

http://www.legaleducation.org.uk/Main/ (25)

Comprehensive information dealing with careers, higher education law degrees and diplomas, pupillage, and BVCs (Bar Vocational Courses), with links to training establishments.

Common Professional Examination (CPE), also known as Postgraduate Diploma in Law (*PGDL*)

http://www.ukcle.ac.uk/directory/cpe.html (26)

A listing of courses available from the UK Centre for Legal Education.

CPE/Diploma in Law Courses

http://www.lawcabs.ac.uk/cpelist.html (27)

This listing has been prepared by the Diploma in Law Courses Central Application Board. For further information see their Home page at *http://www.lawcabs.ac.uk/index.html* (28).

Education (*Legal, by Country*)

http://www.worldlii.org/catalog/2945.html (29)

Provided by the World Legal Information Institute.

European Choice

http://www.dfes.gov.uk/echoice/ (30)

Provided by the Department of Education and Skills, UK, a collation of information on higher education opportunities in European countries. Information on each country provides details on its university structure, linguistic requirements, accommodation, student organisation and services, and a list of relevant Web addresses for seeking further information. Other pages provide information on financial support, useful addresses, and references to relevant printed directories.

HERO (*Higher Education & Research Opportunities in the United Kingdom*)

http://www.hero.ac.uk/ (31)

Extensive information on higher education, including links to the pages of universities and colleges that focus on research (funding, centres, outcomes), studying (applying to universities and colleges, clearing, funding studies), and online prospectuses.

Law Careers Advice Network (*LCAN*)

http://prospects.ac.uk/student/cidd/lcan/Main.htm (32)

'[LCAN] is a partnership of all those involved in providing careers advice to law students and individuals considering a career in law. The network aims to provide all those in search of careers advice with access to current, accurate and realistic careers information, with the Law Society, the General Council of the Bar and the Institute of Legal Executives acting as a central information point.

This site is primarily for undergraduates and graduates, but will be of particular interest to school students.' The site provides information on legal education, training and recruitment, bursaries and scholarships, a good practice guide for the recruitment of solicitors, fact sheets (e.g. on attending career events, financing entry to the bar), and a newsletter.

Law Competitions for Law Students

http://www.law-competitions.com/ (33)

'This gateway site provides links to the websites of national and international legal skills competitions for law students. These are generally not easy to find as they are invariably buried on host universities' websites.' Arranged by country.

Law Degrees in the UK

http://www.ukcle.ac.uk/directory/degrees.html (34)

Links to Home pages provided by the UK Centre for Legal Education. There are also links to listings of part-time degrees, distance and open learning opportunities, and to *senior status* degrees. The latter 'offer an alternative route for non-law graduates, taking two years full time or three years part time'.

OLPAS (*Online Pupillage Application Scheme*)

http://olpas.gti.co.uk/Introduction.asp/ (35)

The scheme requires registration, which is free, and allows applicants to apply to 24 pupillage providers each year on the basis of completing one application form.

Qualifying as a Solicitor

http://www.lawsociety.org.uk/dcs/second_tier.asp?section_id=3/ (36)

Comprehensive information on the requirements and different routes to qualifying as a solicitor in England and Wales, and the requirements, provided by the Law Society. If you have difficulty with the above URL, look for the link *Qualifying as a Solicitor* on their Home page, *http://www.lawsociety.org.uk/* (37).

Scottish Solicitors

http://www.lawscot.org.uk/educ_train/NEW_intro.html (38)

Information on how to become a solicitor entitled to practise in Scotland.

UK Centre for Legal Education

http://www.ukcle.ac.uk/ (39)

Information is provided here on issues relating to the promotion, development and teaching of legal education at both the academic and vocational training stages. This includes news of organised events relating to the provision of legal education and assessment, legal education networks, information on courses in the UK, and issues appertaining to the study of law.

UK Law Schools

http://jurist.law.cam.ac.uk/lawschl.htm (40)

Where available, links are provided to their Home pages, to information on their courses, to prospectuses, and to information on members of staff.

USA Law Schools' Home Pages

http://stu.findlaw.com/schools/fulllist.html (41)

9.4   Courts and tribunals

Court of Justice of the European Communities

http://europa.eu.int/cj/en/index.htm (42)

Information on the workings of the court, and case law. Access to the materials is not very well organised. The link *Case-law* allows users to access full texts by selecting the link *numerical access to the case law*. However, the digest, annotations of judgments, and the alphabetical list are accessed through the link *Research and Documentation*, from the Home page. Parts of the site are still under construction, the bibliography being available only in French (September, 2002).

Court Service Website

http://www.courtservice.gov.uk/ (43)

An agency of the Lord Chancellor's department, this site provides information relating to the courts, tribunals, wills and probate, judgments, daily court listings, daily court status, practice directions, and access to relevant forms, all relating to England and Wales.

Criminal Courts Review/A Review of the Criminal Courts of England and Wales by the Right Honourable Justice Lord Auld, September 2001

http://www.criminal-courts-review.org.uk/ (44)

Employment Appeal Tribunal

http://www.employmentappeals.gov.uk/ (45)

The main category of interest here is the online judgments. The index, left frame, classifies these by type (e.g. disability discrimination), but they can also be searched by EAT no., appellant, respondent, and judge. There is no information as to how far back the archive extends. Forms are available.

European Court of Human Rights

http://www.echr.coe.int/ (46)

Pending cases, judgments and decisions, and basic texts.

Governments on the WWW: Law Courts

http://www.gksoft.com/govt/en/courts.html (47)

Links to judicial institutions arranged by country.

Immigration Appellate Authority

http://www.iaa.gov.uk/ (48)

Information is provided about the IAA, contact addresses of centres, and details of the appeals procedure. Some statistical data is also available.

International Court of Justice

http://www.icj-cij.org/ (49)

Basic documents, practice directions, case law, dockets.

International Courts and Tribunals

http://www.worldlii.org/catalog/2561.html (50)

Links to their Home pages provided by World Legal Information Institute.

International Criminal Court

http://www.un.org/law/icc/index.html (51)

The Rome Statute entered into force in July 2002. The site provides documentation on the UN conference that completed the draft of the statute, on the Preparatory Commission for the court, as well as the text of the statute, the draft text of rules of procedure, and the finalised draft text of the elements of crimes.

International Criminal Tribunal for Rwanda

http://www.ictr.org/ (52)

Governing statutes, procedures and case law.

International Criminal Tribunal for the Former Yugoslavia

http://www.un.org/icty/ (53)

Governing statutes, procedures and case law.

International Tribunal for the Law of the Sea

http://www.itlos.org/ (54)

Lands Tribunal

http://www.courtservice.gov.uk/tribunals/lands_frm.htm (55)

Includes information on its jurisdiction, procedures, practice directions, rules, fees, forms, and decisions. Decisions date back to 1997, but there is no information as to how comprehensive the listing is.

MCSI (*Magistrates Courts Services Inspectorate*) Inspection of Court Services

http://www.mcsi.gov.uk/ (56)

The *Reports and Publications* link provides access to reports on inspections of particular courts, and to thematic reports.

Permanent Court of Arbitration

http://www.pca-cpa.org/ (57)

Privy Council

http://www.privy-council.org.uk/output/page1.asp (58)

Access to Privy Council judgments. When downloaded, only judgments handed down in 2002 were available online (22 August 2002).

Scottish Courts Web Site

http://www.scotcourts.gov.uk/index1.asp (59)

Information on the courts and their procedures, and Court Opinions, divided into two sections, Supreme Court and Sheriff's Courts. Opinions for the latter are only available in relation to significant points of law.

Supreme Court Decisions Around the World

http://www.chanrobles.com/worldjurisprudence.htm (60)

Arranged by country. The term 'supreme court' is somewhat problematically deployed as for some countries the link is to of sources of high court judgments, or judgments at various levels of the judicial system, including the highest court.

Tribunals

http://www.courtservice.gov.uk/tribunals/tribs_home.htm (61)

Part of the Court Service Web site (*see* above). Information and decisions relating to the Employment Appeal Tribunal (*see* above), Immigration Appellate

Authority (*see* above), Lands Tribunal (*see* above), Tax Appeal Tribunal, Social Security and Child Support Commissioners, VAT and Duties Tribunal, Special Commissioners and Financial Services and Market Tribunals. Selected decisions are available.

Tribunals for Users – One System, One Service. Report of the Review of Tribunals by Sir Andrew Legatt, March 2001

http://www.courtservice.gov.uk/tribunals/rev_frm.htm (62)

9.5 Directories

ABA Network Lawyer Locator

http://lawyers.martindale.com/php/aba/Lawyer.php3 (63)

A service of the American Bar Association. Note the onsite recommendation: 'it is important, before hiring any lawyer, to contact the lawyer disciplinary agency in the state where the lawyer maintains a business address to confirm that the individual is in good standing as a member of the bar.' An online listing of each state's lawyer disciplinary agency may be found at *http://www.abanet.org/cpr/disciplinary.html* (64).

Faculty of Advocates – Practising Members

http://www.advocates.org.uk/web/surname.htm (65)

Contact information for those independent lawyers who have been admitted to practise as Advocates before the courts of Scotland.

Judiciary (England and Wales) – Senior Judiciary List

http://www.lcd.gov.uk/judicial/senjudfr.htm (66)

Judges of the United States Courts

http://air.fjc.gov/history/judges_frm.html (67)

This database, provided by the Federal Judicial Center, includes information on the service record and biographical information for all judges who have served on the US District Courts, Circuit Courts, Courts of Appeals, and the Supreme Court since 1789. The information is updated regularly.

Law Firms on the Web

http://www.lawontheweb.co.uk/lawyers-find.htm (68)

Search engine allows for searches by key word (name of firm), geographical area, specialism, town, and postcode.

Law Society of Scotland – All Solicitors

http://www.lawscot.org.uk/all.html (69)

Contact information for all solicitors of the Law Society of Scotland who hold practising certificates. Can be searched by location, surname, and firm name.

LawyerLocator UK

http://www.lawyerlocator.co.uk/ (70)

Free listing of solicitors, including Scottish. For advanced searching select the *Legal Professionals Area* button.

Legal500.com: The International Centre for Commercial Law

http://www.legal500.com/index.php (71)

This is a very useful directory, principally listing practitioners of commercial law. It includes information on both UK- and foreign-based firms, and, as far as the UK is concerned, on both solicitors firms and chambers. There is a lot of useful information relating to firms outside the UK, grouped by region and country, but considerations of space prevent detailing here.

Selecting the link UK brings up a menu that links to *Recommended Firms*, a listing of which can be obtained by selecting a region from the map that downloads. Having done that, you select a specialism (e.g. insurance, real estate), which will download a listing of firms in the region providing services in this field. At the top of the listing is an overview of the region, a section on *Regional heavyweights* and on *Leading individuals*. When you get to the Home pages of the firms you can obtain a *Profile* of particular firms, a listing of their partners, career information on particular partners, an analysis of the type of work undertaken by the firm, and information on its *Size*, which details the number of partners, assistants, etc. Instead of locating firms/individuals via the image map, there is also an alphabetical law firm directory.

From the UK Home page, there is also a link to leading barristers' chambers, information on in-house lawyers, which provides information relating to in-house counsel and departments, size and fees tables.

This is a resource that includes a substantial volume of information, which justifies some time spent in exploring its various facets. Although nominally it deals with commercial law, many firms that practise this also handle other types of cases, and the information on particular individuals and firms provides details, *inter alia*, on other work carried out.

Martindale-Hubbell at lawyers.com

http://www.lawyers.com/ (72)

Directory of US lawyers. You can filter by type of lawyer/law and location, and can also search by name.

Queens Counsel – Appointments and Applications

http://www.lcd.gov.uk/judicial/qcinfofr.htm (73)

Listings and statistics on the relationship between applications and appointments, from 1998.

Solicitors Online

http://www.solicitors-online.com/ (74)

Search engine provided by the Law Society, which represents the interests of solicitors in England and Wales. The search engine allows users to locate individual solicitors, law firms, Registered European Lawyers (an EU lawyer working in England and Wales and registered with the Society), and Registered Foreign Lawyers. You can filter by various criteria, including the name of the solicitor or firm, subject specialisms, the availability of legal aid or a fixed fee interview, location, and whether or not the firm provides training contracts. One drawback to the service is that it is necessary to know the name of the area of the city in which the firm/solicitor is located, and, preferably, the postcode.

State Court Locator

http://vls.law.vill.edu/Locator/statecourt/ (75)

Provided by the Villanova University School of Law, links to the Home pages of state courts in the USA, and to applicable case law. If links to opinions are not separately listed, refer to the Home pages of the courts.

Universal Citation

http://www.abanet.org/tech/ltrc/research/citation/ (76)

Links to citation guides for the USA, Australia, Canada, and the UK, provided by the American Bar Association.

Waterlow's Barristers Directory

http://www.connectinglegal.com/indexbarristers.htm (77)

Searchable fields are chambers name, town, county, postcode, and work description.

Waterlow's Solicitors Directory

http://www.connectinglegal.com/indexsolicitors.htm (78)

Searchable fields are firm name, town, county, postcode, work category, number of partners, and language.

9.6　Legal research

American Society of International Law: Guide to Electronic Resources for International Law

http://www.asil.org/resource/home.htm (79)

A large collection of detailed annotated links. The main headings under which they are grouped include human rights, international commercial arbitration, international criminal law, international economic law, international environmental law, and private international law. Includes information on research strategies, library materials, bibliographies, periodical literature, and similar.

Australian Guide to Legal Citation

http://www.law.unimelb.edu.au/mulr/aglc.htm (80)

The guide, which is in PDF format and can be downloaded, is published by the Melbourne Law Review Association. In addition to outlining the system of citation for Australian materials, it reviews suggestions for citing materials from Canada, New Zealand, the UK, and the USA.

English Law Guide

http://libwww.essex.ac.uk/LAW/englawguide.html (81)

Although aimed at undergraduate students at the University of Essex, this guide lists resources that LLB degree students elsewhere will most probably find useful. Many of the electronic resources that are referenced in the guide as being accessible to Essex students are likely to be available to students at other institutions of higher education in the UK.

European Union Law Information Resources

http://www.lawschool.cornell.edu/library/guides/eu/eu.html (82)

Provided by Cornell University Law Library, a brief overview of EU institutions and sources of law with links.

FLAG (*Foreign Law Guide*)

http://193.62.18.223/dbtw-wpd/textbase/collsearch.htm (83)

This is an online search engine of a database of international comparative law collections held within UK university and national libraries. The database can be searched by country (jurisdiction, e.g. Oregon) or the name of an international organisation, type of legal literature (e.g. court reports, treaties), the regional location in the UK of contributing (depository) libraries. According to SOSIG 'FLAG holds over 11,000 collection records covering more than 50 UK libraries including law libraries in Universities and research institutes, the British Library, the Advocates Library, and the National Library of Wales. The collections described in the database relate to over 250 jurisdictions world-wide (excluding the United Kingdom), UK devolved jurisdictions, and the European Union.'

Foreign Legal Research – A Selective List of Guides

http://library.law.columbia.edu/foreignguide.html (84)

Provided by Columbia University Library, arranged by region and country.

Foreign Primary Law on the Web

http://www.law.uh.edu/librarians/tmulligan/foreignlaw.html (85)

Provided by the University of Houston Law Center, arranged by country, detailing whether the text is available in the language of origin or in English translation.

Guide to European Union Legal Research

*http://www.law.harvard.edu/library/ref/ils_ref/eu_guide/
eu_legal_research.htm* (86)

Provided by Harvard University Law Library, this is a useful and comprehensive summary of resources with links. The sections include EU documentation sources, legislation, European Parliament documents, an extensive bibliography, and information on the resources available via the databases of Westlaw and Lexis.

Guide to International Refugee Law Resources on the Web

http://www.llrx.com/features/refugee.htm (87)

Compiled by Elisa Mason, who worked for six years with the UN High Commissioner for Refugees (UNHCR), published July 2000.

Guide to Law Online

http://www.loc.gov/law/guide/index.html (88)

Provided by the US Library of Congress. Resources arranged under: international and multinational, nations of the world, US Federal, and US states and territories.

Guide to UK Legal System

http://www.llrx.com/features/uk2.htm (89)

Provided by Sarah Carter, Law Librarian at the University of Kent, Canterbury.

Harvard Law School Research Guides

http://www.law.harvard.edu/library/research_guides/research_page.htm
(90)

The guides are grouped under general library, Anglo-American law, international, foreign and comparative law, and electronic resources research guides.

How to Publish in Top Journals

http://www.ag.iastate.edu/journals/rie/how.htm (91)

Written by Kwan Choi, some good advice and worrying information about how long you may wait to see your brilliance in print. Although written by an economist, and providing examples relating to that field, much of the detail and advice can be generalised to other discipline areas.

International Commercial Arbitration: Locating the Resources

http://www.llrx.com/features/arbitration2.htm (92)

Compiled by Jean M. Wenger, who is the Government Documents/Foreign & International Law Librarian at Cook County Law Library, a practitioner's library in Chicago.

International Criminal Law: A Selective Resource Guide

http://www.llrx.com/features/int_crim3.htm (93)

Prepared by M. J. Raisch and G. Partin. Covers history, international criminal courts and tribunals, extradition and mutual assistance, specific crimes (crimes against humanity and human rights, organised crime and narcotics, terrorism and piracy, cyber-crime), and crime prevention and criminal justice.

International Environmental Law Research Guide

http://www.ll.georgetown.edu/intl/guides/environment/ (94)

Prepared by Georgetown University law library. Sections include bibliographies and research guides, background and general sources, treaties, national and international statutes, and national and international case law.

International Family Law

http://www.llrx.com/features/int_fam.htm (95)

Compiled by Marylin Johnson Raisch, Librarian for International and Foreign Law at the Bora Laskin Law Library of the University of Toronto Faculty of Law.

International Law Research Guides

http://library.law.columbia.edu/intlaw.html (96)

Provided by the Library, Columbia University Law School, a series of guides, including treaty research, EU legal materials, United Nations, and public international law.

Introduction to Basic Legal Citation (*2000–2001 edn.*)

http://www.hg.org/cgi-bin/redir.cgi?url=http://www.law.cornell.edu:80/ citation/citation.table.html (97)

Provided by Peter W. Martin, Cornell Law School. This extensive presentation is based on the American, *Bluebook*, system.

Law Reports – *The Times*

http://www.timesonline.co.uk/ (98)

From the panel on the left select *Law*, then *Law Reports*. Reports dating from October 2000 were available (August 2002).

Legal Resources in Europe

http://www.jura.uni-sb.de/english/euro.html (99)

Provided from the University of Saarbrücken, links to the Council of Europe and EU institutions, and to law resources for EU countries and non-EU European countries.

Legal Writing

http://www.ncl.ac.uk/nuls/lectures/legwrit/citation.htm (100)

A detailed discussion of the system of legal citation in the UK, by Bruce Grant, Newcastle Law School, University of Newcastle upon Tyne.

Nations of the World: Guide to Law Online

http://www.loc.gov/law/guide/nations.html (101)

Provided by the US Library of Congress, arranged by country. Extensive links, arranged under: constitution, executive, judicial, legislative, legal guides, and general sources.

Research Guides

http://www.law.duke.edu/lib/research_guide.html (102)

Published by the Law Library, Duke University, a useful series of guides, divided into foreign and international, and US materials. The former includes Canadian legal research, English law, Council of Europe, EU, international law, and UN.

US materials include sections on court rules, directories of courts and judges, federal legislative history, federal administrative law, and legal ethics. The guides are clearly written and provide links to related resources.

Researching Foreign and International Law

http://www.ll.georgetown.edu/intl/guides/ (103)

Provided by the University of Georgetown Law Library. It includes a very detailed tutorial on *International Legal Research*. Although this makes reference in the second page of the introduction to the Georgetown University library collection, don't be put off by this. The tutorial references numerous Internet sources, as well as Westlaw and Lexis.

There are three other collections of research guides. The first, *Basics*, includes *Basics of International and Foreign Legal Research, Introduction to International Legal Research, Researching Foreign and Comparative Law*, and *Treaty Research*. The second, *Methods*, consists of *English Language Sources, Locating Journal Articles on Foreign and International Law and Related Topics*, and *Using Electronic Resources*. The latter advises on the use of Internet resources, CD-ROMs, Westlaw, and Lexis. The third collection consists of research guides on particular topics, of which there are a large number. The 20 areas listed include: antitrust law, comparative constitutional law, immigration and human rights resources on the Internet, refugee protection, and trade law.

There are also four Internet Resource Collections: *Researching International Economic Law on the Internet, Environmental Law Web Sites, Foreign Law on the Web*, and *International Law Links*, all of which provide links to resources in these fields available on the Web.

All in all, this is an excellent collection of research guides and resources.

Rights International Research Guide for International Human Rights Lawyers

http://www.rightsinternational.org/links.html (104)

An extensive guide to both online and printed sources, dated July 2000.

Starting Research in UK Law

http://www.lib.gla.ac.uk/Docs/Research/uklaw.html (105)

Provided by Glasgow University library. Subjects covered include primary sources, secondary sources, statutory instruments, and cases. Linked to Internet resources where applicable/appropriate.

United Nations Documentation Research Guide on Human Rights

http://www.un.org/Depts/dhl/resguide/spechr.htm (106)

A guide to the documents produced by UN human rights bodies.

9.7 Legal systems

American Legal System – Introductory Overview

http://www.cec.org/pubs_info_resources/law_treat_agree/
summary_enviro_law/publication/us01.cfm?varlan=english (107)

A useful introductory overview provided by the North American Commission for Environmental Cooperation, with links to relevant materials. Sections: structure of government, federal government, sub-national governments, sources and hierarchy of law, role of the legislature and the executive, role of the courts, legal instruments.

Australia's Legal System

http://law.gov.au/auslegalsys/auslegalsys.htm (108)

Overview provided by the Australian Attorney General's Department. See also *Australian Law on the Internet **http://www.nla.gov.au/oz/law.html*** (109).

Canadian Legal System – Introductory Overview

http://www.cec.org/pubs_info_resources/law_treat_agree/
summary_enviro_law/publication/ca01.cfm?varlan=english (110)

An overview that parallels in its subject content that provided by the North American Commission for Environmental Cooperation on the American legal system (*see* above).

People's Republic of China: Laws and Legal System

http://www.qis.net/chinalaw/prexp2.htm (111)

Provided by the University of Maryland, a collation of links to articles dealing with various facets of law and the legal system in China, but including also some materials relating to conducting business there. See also the section on the Special Administrative Region of Hong Kong, at ***http://www.qis.net/chinalaw/explnhk.htm*** (112).

Scotland: A Guide to Scots Law

http://www.law.gla.ac.uk/scot_guide/ToC.HTML (113)

The guide appears to have been authored by Evi C. Athanasekou, Department of Computing Science, University of Glasgow.

9.8   Mailing lists

CISNEWS

http://www.cis.org/mail_login.html (114)

This is the URL to access to subscribe to the mailing list provided by the *Center for Immigration Studies*, a non-profit research organisation based in Washington, DC. The mailing list, which has some 5000 subscribers, provides information on immigration news from around the world, in the form of two postings a day, one dealing with the US, and the other non-US territories. The Center, *http://www.cis.org/* (115), also publishes various reports.

Employment Law (UK) Mailing List

http://www.danielbarnett.co.uk/list2.html (116)

Managed by Daniel Barnett, Barrister, the list had some 4650 subscribers in June 2002, most of whom specialise in employment law. The list provides bulletins that are sent out each week detailing new legislation and significant employment law cases.

9.9   Miscellaneous

Stephen's Guide to Logical Fallacies

http://www.datanation.com/fallacies/ (117)

Compiled by Stephen Downes, University of Alberta, the site provides examples of logical fallacies, and mistakes of reasoning, divided into 13 categories. All are accompanied by examples and are referenced. Examples are: fallacies of distraction/false dilemma: *Either you are for me or you are against me*; inductive/false analogy: *Employees are like nails. Just as nails must be hit in the head in order to make them work, so must employees*; syllogistic fallacies/illicit major: *All Texans are Americans, and no Californians are Texans, therefore, no Californians are Americans.*

9.10   Positions

Chronicle of Higher Education

http://chronicle.com/jobs/ (118)

Extensive listing of positions in colleges and universities (faculty, administrative, technical, executive), primarily, but not exclusively, in the USA.

Fish

http://www.fish4.co.uk (119)

Provided by a consortium of national and local newspapers. Easy-to-use search engine: select type of job and location. Database included 38,500+ entries, 14 June 2002.

Government Legal Service

http://www.gls.gov.uk/ (120)

UK government legal positions recruitment Web site.

jobs.ac.uk

http://www.jobs.ac.uk/ (121)

Online employment bulletin for academic positions, mainly based in the UK, but some in commonwealth countries. Filtering available by institution type, discipline, sub-discipline, location, and contract type (permanent, etc.).

Jobs4law

http://www.jobs4law.net/ (122)

A service of *Legal Week*, *http://www.legalit.net/* (123).

Jobs in Law

http://www.jobsin.co.uk/law/index.html (124)

Law Careers.Net

http://www.lawcareers.net/lcn.asp (125)

In addition to a listing of immediate vacancies, there is information on solicitors and barristers, training contracts, training contract deadlines, vacation scheme deadlines and searches, and pupillage search. Details are also available on courses: undergraduate, CPE, PGDL, LPC, and BVC.

Law Gazette

http://www.lawgazette.co.uk/jobsearch/jobsearchframe.asp (126)

Substantial number of offers for various legal job titles.

Monster

http://www.monster.co.uk/ (127)

Claims to have details of over 1 million jobs globally, 19,000+ in the UK, 60,000+ in Europe (14 June 2002). There are facilities for creating and leaving your CV in the database for potential employers to pick out and contact you, or, alternatively, you can interrogate the database for suitable employment opportunities that you can apply for. In tracking down jobs you select the region where you are interested in working, then the type of employment.

Telegraph Jobs

http://www.jobs.telegraph.co.uk (128)

Provided by the *Telegraph* newspaper, tends to be skewed towards executive positions, but there are enough available at the middle to lower end of the remuneration scale to justify a search. Use the *Matrix* option to choose region and salary. You can also search by employer and field of employment. Database is not large.

TES (*Times Educational Supplement*)/Jobs

http://www.tesjobs.co.uk/ (129)

The Lawyer Group

http://www.thelawyer.com/LawyerJobs/ (130)

A substantial listing of law-related employment opportunities.

THES (*Times Higher Education Supplement*)/Jobs

http://www.jobs.thes.co.uk/ (131)

9.11 Practitioners

See 9.5 Directories

9.12 Professional conduct

American Legal Ethics Library

http://www.law.cornell.edu/ethics/ (132)

'This digital library contains both the codes or rules setting standards for the professional conduct of lawyers and commentary on the law governing lawyers, organized on a state by state basis.'

ETHICSearch

http://www.abanet.org/cpr/ethicsearch/home.html (133)

Resources on professional ethics provided by the American Bar Association.

Law Society Guide to the Professional Conduct of Solicitors

http://www.guide-on-line.lawsociety.org.uk/ (134)

Comprehensive online guide.

9.13 Publications

(1) Articles/journals

All Academic

http://www.allacademic.com/journal_list.html (135)

A listing of links to full-text online journals and magazines arranged by subject areas.

Contents Pages from Law Reviews and Other Scholarly Journals

http://tarlton.law.utexas.edu/tallons/content_search.html (136)

Provided by the Tarlton Law Library, University of Texas, current contents pages of more than 750 journals. You can either type in the name of the journal in the search text box, or browse the list, which is sub-divided into those published in and outside the USA.

Electronic Journals Resource Directory

http://library.usask.ca/~scottp/links/ (137)

Compiled by Peter Scott, University of Saskatchewan Libraries, the resource provides links under various categories that facilitate the location of electronic journals. These include general electronic journal indexes, library databases of electronic journals, library-related journals dealing with electronic journals, mailing lists for discussing electronic journals, and publishers of electronic journals. If you wish to locate electronic journals dealing with general or specific legal topics, this is a good place to start.

Find Articles

http://www.findarticles.com/PI/index.jhtml (138)

This database includes articles from more than 300 journals and magazines, dating from 1998, and is available free of charge; the term *law* returned 124,877, tort 40,568, and contributory negligence 2394 entries, respectively (12 August 2002).

Ingenta (*previously Carl Uncover*)

http://www.ingenta.com/ (139)

This database, which is the most efficient that I am familiar with on the Web, included, on 12 August 2002, references to 13,143,502 articles published in

27,178 publications. Searching is free, and most articles can be purchased for the fees specified, sent the same day by fax or electronic mail. The search engine allows for queries by title, keyword and abstract, by author name, and by publication title, which can be filtered by volume, issue, year, and *since date*. Select the *search options* from the Home page. The database starting date is 1988.

The facility provides an easily navigable means of searching for publications by subject, journal, year, and issue. Owing to the size of the database, many entries will span tens of pages. You can mark articles of interest, or complete lists, for retrieval by electronic mail. Many of the articles are available online to subscribers, and queries can be targeted on the complete database, or just on those that are available for reading/downloading online, to institutional subscribers.

There is also a listing of online journals with links to their current and past issues. To access those categorised under *law*, select from the page, the pages *Social Sciences*, then *Law*, then *online journals*, in succession.

International Law Journals

http://august1.com/pubs/dict/j.htm#journals (140)

Journals are available online except where it is indicated that abstracts or selected articles only are freely available electronically.

Law Gazette

http://www.lawgazette.co.uk/homeframe.asp (141)

Official publication of the Law Society.

Law Reviews

http://jurist.law.pitt.edu/lawrev.htm (142)

Links to the Home pages of 350+ law journals with substantial online content, from *Jurist* (*http://jurist.law.pitt.edu/*) (143).

Law Reviews and Journals

http://www.chanrobles.com/lawreview.htm (144)

This is a lengthy list of 'Law-Related E-Journals and Periodicals' provided by the Chan Robles Virtual Law Library, a Philippine online resource provided by the Chan Robles Group. Some of the links no longer work but many of them do. The list is more comprehensive than others I have managed to locate. It seems to be accurate in respect of whether current issues are accessible online. I found that typing in the journal title in the Google toolbar (or the Google search engine if you do not have this installed), when the link provided was dead, invariably located the new URL, e.g. *Temple Law Review*.

Law Reviews Online

http://www.loc.gov/law/guide/lawreviews.html (145)

Provided by the US Library of Congress. Links to 'electronic law journals and other periodicals providing substantial amounts of legal analysis are included below. Listings include those sites offering free and complete access to the full text of articles and notes. Journals which offer only promotional information, tables of contents, or abstracts are omitted.'

New Jour

http://gort.ucsd.edu/newjour/ (146)

This is a mailing list (subscription address: *listproc@ccat.sas.upenn.edu*) for the announcement of new journals, digests, and serials available electronically on the Internet. Its main interest lies in its searchable archive, which dates from 1993, accessed by selecting *Search*. You can query the text of messages sent to the journal or search for keywords in the titles of journals. This is a very useful resource for tracking down electronic journals dealing with particular subjects. From the records retrieved there is a link to a details record that provides information on the journal, including the subjects that it deals with, the target audience, its relevance to readers with particular interests, place of publication, and links to the publisher and/or online Home page. This information also details whether the publication is available freely, or only to subscribers of the print journal, if applicable. The drawback with online archives, of course, is that many of the URLs referenced may have changed or the services/resources advertised may no longer be available.

The Lawyer

http://www.the-lawyer.co.uk/ (147)

Online magazine for lawyers, covers news items, events, and jobs.

(2) Books/bibliographies/papers/reviews

Books-On-Law

http://jurist.law.pitt.edu/lawbooks/index.htm (148)

In-depth reviews of books on law related topics provided by *Jurist*. Reviews are archived from 1999. As *Jurist* is an American site, those reviewed tend towards American law and the interests of US practitioners and social scientists.

House of Commons Library Research Papers

http://www.parliament.uk/commons/lib/research/rpintro.htm (149)

Papers on subjects of contemporary political interest to members of parliament compiled by the staff of the House of Commons Library. Papers available date from 1998.

International Criminal Court: Resources in Print and Electronic Format

http://www.lib.uchicago.edu/~llou/icc.html (150)

Provided by the library of the University of Chicago. Updated regularly.

Personal Guide to Know How for Family Lawyers: Text books and suggested bibliography

http://www.briefjacquig.co.uk/articleformatter.php?filelocation=articles/ 020325025134.html (151)

Compiled by Jacqui Gilliatt, Barrister.

Working Papers

http://jurist.law.pitt.edu/ol_artcl.htm (152)

Links to a collection of working papers provided by *Jurist*. See also links to faculty and law professors' Home pages at ***http://jurist.law.pitt.edu/ home_pgs.htm*** (153), as many online publications of individual scholars are listed here.

(3) Dissertations

Dissertation Abstracts

http://wwwlib.umi.com/dissertations/search (154)

This database includes some 1.6 million dissertation abstracts from North American universities, dating from 1861. Free searching is only available for the past two years, access to other years being dependent on institutional subscription. The basic search engine permits queries on a number of fields, including author, date frame, ISBN, and keyword. For each entry returned you can view the abstract, or a 24-page preview. The dissertations can be ordered, the cheapest version being emailed in PDF format, at surprisingly low costs. The cost of a PhD dissertation, regardless of size, was $25 (February 2002). Currently, PDF format is only available for post-1996 dissertations.

Index to Theses

http://www.theses.com/ (155)

The database covers theses accepted from 1970 to 2001 in UK institutions of higher education and research centres. It is available to institutions and individuals that subscribe to the print edition. Generally, therefore, it is available through the libraries of most institutions of higher education in the UK.

(4) Publishers

Her Majesty's Stationery Office

http://www.hmso.gov.uk/ (156)

Official publications of the UK Government and Legislature.

Publishers Catalogues

http://www.lights.com/publisher/ (157)

The 7400+ entries can be searched by publisher's name, country or city location, or by browsing the index. There are also entries by topic and type of material (books, magazines, ebooks, etc.). Entries link to publisher's Web sites.

9.14 Reference materials

(1) Acronyms, abbreviations, glossaries

Abbreviations

http://www.reliefweb.int/help/abbrev.html (158)

Provided by the UN ReliefWeb, an extensive listing.

Acronym Database

http://www.ucc.ie/acronyms/ (159)

Acronyms and abbreviations

http://www.ucc.ie/cgi-bin/acronym (160)

Acronym Search

http://www.acronymsearch.com/ (161)

Acronyms/Subjects: The Opaui Guide to Lists of Acronyms, Abbreviations and Initialisms

http://www.opaui.com/acro.html (162)

Arranged by subject fields (e.g. accountancy, genetics, legal).

Bluebook Abbreviations of Law Review Titles

http://lib.law.washington.edu/cilp/abbrev.html (163)

Glossary of the European Communities and European Union

http://info.abdn.ac.uk/pir/sources/eurogide.htm (164)

Glossarist

http://www.glossarist.com/ (165)

A search engine for glossaries.

Legal Abbreviations

http://library.ukc.ac.uk/library/info/subjectg/law/abbrev.htm (166)

'A list of common legal abbreviations, including law report series and legal journals, as well as a few general abbreviations commonly used in law.'

(2) Banks

Department for Education and Skills (*UK*) Student Support

http://www.dfes.gov.uk/studentsupport/ (167)

Money Supermarket

http://www.moneysupermarket.com/ (168)

This site provides comparative information on overdrafts, insurance policies, travel insurance, etc.

Student Loans Company Limited

http://www.slc.co.uk/ (169)

UK Banks and Building Societies

http://bubl.ac.uk/uk/banks.htm (170)

(3) Biographical

Biographical Dictionary

http://www.s9.com/biography/ (171)

28,000 entries. No hypertext cross-referencing.

Biography.com

http://www.biography.com/ (172)

25,000 cross-referenced biographies. Some external links also.

Lives, the Biography Resource

http://amillionlives.com/ (173)

A meta-biographical resource that links individual names to biographical data uploaded elsewhere on servers. This means that for some individuals there are links to more than one biographical entry. There are also links to various specialist biographical collections (e.g. African Americans, Women, the Holocaust, American Civil War, the Professions).

(4) Country information

Area Studies

http://www.psr.keele.ac.uk/area.htm (174)

Provided by Richard Kimber, links to online resources dealing with political related issues, organised by country. The volume of resources linked to varies by country, but most include links to official pages of that country, its constitution, and election information.

Background by Country

http://www.reliefweb.int/w/rwb.nsf/vBkC (175)

Provided by the United Nations' *ReliefWeb*, this site provides links to information on member states under a large number of headings, including history, demographics, development, government and politics, economics, travel information, and culture.

Background Notes

http://www.state.gov/www/background_notes/ (176)

Provided by the US Department of State. Authoritative schematic information available on geography, people, history, government, economy, principal government officials, political conditions, foreign relations, defence, and travel and business information.

Country Indicators for Foreign Policy: Country Ranking Tables

http://www.carleton.ca/cifp/rank.htm#RANK (177)

This site ranks countries in tabular form on a large number of variables. The main headings, which are further sub-divided, include history of armed conflict, governance and political instability (level of democracy, regime durability, restrictions on civil rights), militarisation (military expenditure, armed forces), population and heterogeneity, demographic stress, economic performance, human development, and environmental stress. It is necessary to review the page on *Indicator Descriptions* to interpret the comparative rankings. The articles linked to from the *Methodology Reports* page may also be of some interest.

CountryReports.Org

http://www.CountryReports.Org (178)

Provides useful outline information by country on its economy, people, defense, geography, government, history, and includes related links under various headings. Also included are well-produced maps.

Ethnologue.com

http://www.ethnologue.com/country_index.asp (179)

Arranged by country, this well-organised and informative site provides details on size of population groups, and the languages spoken by its inhabitants. Details of the numbers speaking each language are provided. There is further information on each language, providing details of where else that language is spoken.

European Forum Country Updates

http://www.europeanforum.net/cup/country.htm (180)

Provides information on the political situation in eastern European countries and the Russian Federation. For most entries the headings include: basic facts (population, GNP, etc.), the economic situation, the political situation (developments since 1989, elections and composition of government, etc.), the political landscape (political parties, labour unions, etc.), and sources of further information.

FIRST (*Facts on International Relations and Security Trends*)

http://first.sipri.org/ (181)

This is an integrated database system that allows users to select a variety of variables relating to between one and six countries at any one time. The main areas covered include government memberships and agreements, military expenditure, nuclear weapons and ballistic missiles, country indicators and statistics, armed forces, conventional weapons holdings, and military activities. The data is drawn from a number of sources (e.g. Bonn International Centre for Conversion). It is also possible to retrieve information under any number of headings for a particular country. The information is reasonably detailed and well presented.

Global Statistics

http://www.xist.org/index.htm (182)

This site is primarily useful for information relating to the population of countries, cities, and geographical areas. Provides information on historical demographic changes, and future projections. Information is culled from official sources, primarily the UN. Also includes information on economic development. The Global Data Index *http://www.xist.org/global/ixgd.htm* (183), provides a statistical overview, whereas the Country Data Index, *http://www.xist.org/cd/ixcd.htm* (184), as the title implies, focuses on details for each country.

Handbook of International Economic Statistics

http://www.odci.gov/cia/di/products/hies/index.html (185)

Produced by the US Central Intelligence Agency (CIA), this version dates from February 1999. It is in PDF format, so you will need the Adobe reader. The charts are in Excel format. If your browser cannot open them, right click with the mouse, save to disk, and bring up in Excel, or configure your browser to automatically open Excel for files with an xls extension. The 1998 version is in HTML format, and can be accessed from *http://www.odci.gov/cia/publications/hies97/b/b.htm* (186). The time frame is 1970 to the date of publication, and 267 nations are covered.

Human Rights Reports

http://www.state.gov/g/drl/rls/hrrpt/ (187)

These are produced annually by the US Department of State under the provisions of the Foreign Assistance Act of 1961, and amendments thereto. Arranged by country, they provide useful information, not only on the human rights situation, but also on the general political situation and structure in each. Those for 1999–2001 are available online at this site. Reports for 1993–1998 are available at *http://www.state.gov/www/global/human_rights/hrp_reports_mainhp.html* (188).

INCORE Internet Country Guides

http://www.incore.ulst.ac.uk/cds/countries/ (189)

Information on Internet resources on conflict and ethnicity in relation to countries currently, or recently, subject to major internal conflicts. The categories under which the resources are arranged include email lists, news sources, non-governmental organisations, and maps.

Library of Congress Country Studies

http://memory.loc.gov/frd/cs/cshome.html (190)

The Web version of a series originally published in hardback by the Federal Research Division. It provides information by country on 'the historical setting and the social, economic, political, and national security systems and institutions of countries throughout the world and examines the interrelationships of those systems and the ways they are shaped by cultural factors'. The information provided is quite extensive, and relates to geography, demographics, religion, security and military, government, and economy, among other categories.

Political Reference Almanac – Nations of the World

http://www.polisci.com/almanac/nations/entities.htm (191)

Provided by PoliSci.com, the summary table provides information on population size, area, and heads of government. If you select the link to the country name, more general information is provided, as is a list of members of the executive and the offices they hold, schematic information relating to the legislature, the judiciary, local government, the economy, and the major international organisations that the country belongs to. There is also information on the latest election results and the number of those elected from each party. The material is well organised and presented.

World Desk Reference

http://travel.dk.com/wdr/index.htm (192)

Provides outline information on countries under numerous headings, including maps, transportation, tourism, politics, defence, and resources.

World Factbook 2001

http://www.cia.gov/cia/publications/factbook/index.html (193)

An annual publication compiled by the US CIA, with an entry for each country that provides useful and quite extensive information relating to its economic, political, and institutional circumstances. Information is available on major political institutions, basic demographic information, names of members of the government at the time of writing, a listing of the main political parties and their leaders, and similar. Also included is a map for each country, details on the economy, a brief listing of current international disputes the country is involved in, information on its defence forces and expenditures, date on infrastructure, and much else besides. A linked document explains the methodology of its compilation. For subsequent and previous years reports enter the query *World Factbook year* in the search engine Google, or access from ***http://www.umsl.edu/ services/govdocs/index.html#alphalist*** (194).

World Time Server

http://www.worldtimeserver.com/ (195)

Times for locations worldwide. Select the location, and the current time relative to your own is provided. You can also enter information relating to different locations at some future date.

World Law

http://jurist.law.pitt.edu/world/index.htm (196)

Provided by *Jurist*. Country listing that provides, for most, information on the constitution, government and legislation, courts and judgments, human rights, the legal profession, and law schools.

(5) Dictionaries – general

AskOxford.com

http://www.askoxford.com/ (197)

Oxford Paperback Dictionary and Thesaurus.

Cambridge Dictionaries Online

http://dictionary.cambridge.org/ (198)

Dictionaries on the Web

http://www.helsinki.fi/~hkantola/dict.html (199)

Dictionaries by language of translation from – (primarily) into English, but many others as well (e.g. Danish–Japanese). This is a very large file and may take a long time to download on slow connections. It may be quicker to enter a query in Google (e.g. Danish–Japanese Dictionary).

Foreignword.com

http://www.ctv.es/USERS/alberfon/dicsear1.htm (200)

Translates from 67 source languages into 69 target languages. There is also a facility for translating small portions of text.

Merriam-Webster (*US Spelling*)

http://www.m-w.com/dictionary.htm (201)

Based on the 10th Collegiate, 1993 edition. It includes 160,000+ entries.

(6) Dictionaries – legal

Cyberlaw Encyclopedia

http://www.gahtan.com/cyberlaw/ (202)

Duhaime's Law Dictionary

http://www.duhaime.org/diction.htm (203)

Encyclopedia of Law and Economics

http://allserv.rug.ac.be/~gdegeest/ (204)

'The Encyclopedia of *Law and Economics* is a . . . reference work that attempts to survey the whole law and economics literature in nearly 5,000 pages. Most entries contain two elements: a review of the literature, written by an authority in the field, and a quasi complete bibliography (not just a selection).'

International Law Dictionary and Directory

http://august1.com/pubs/dict/contrib.htm (205)

'Definitions of words and phrases used in private and public international law with linked cross-references to related words and phrases.'

lawdictionaries.com

http://www.lawdictionaries.com/ (206)

Links to law dictionaries classified under: general, commercial, crime and human rights, family and alternative dispute procedure, international law, and other. A very useful resource.

The 'Lectric Law Library's Legal Lexicon's Lyceum

http://www.lectlaw.com/def.htm (207)

(7) General

NGO directory

http://www.un.org/MoreInfo/ngolink/ngodir.htm (208)

NIRA's World Directory of Think Tanks

http://www.nira.go.jp/ice/tt-info/nwdtt99/ (209)

xrefer

http://www.xrefer.com/about.jsp (210)

This search engine database consists of some 50 UK reference resources, including language and specialist dictionaries, which can be used for keyword searching, or keyword searches by subject area. The title list of database texts includes entries under art, encyclopedias, English literature, health, philosophy, science, quotations, and thesaurus.

(8) Libraries

British Library Newspaper Library Web Catalogue

http://www.bl.uk/collections/newspaper/newscat.html (211)

The catalogue 'includes entries for over 50,000 newspaper and periodical titles from all over the world, dating from the 17th to the 21st century, held by the British Library Newspaper Library at Colindale in north west London. Catalogue entries contain full details of the title (including any title changes), the place of publication (the town or city and the country), and the dates which are held, and the catalogue may be searched by entering a keyword or a combination of keywords.'

British Library Public Catalogue

http://blpc.bl.uk/ (212)

The main UK national depository library. The online catalogue provides details of more than 10 million books. It is a major resource for tracking books by subject, for checking publisher particulars for referencing, and for establishing whether the library holds particular items that can be made available through the inter-library loan provisions applicable to institutions of higher education in the UK.

COPAC

http://copac.ac.uk/copac/wzgw?db=copact (213)

A search engine interface that enables users to query the combined online catalogues of libraries of the Consortium of University Research Libraries (UK). The combined databases can be searched by author and by subject, and there is also a periodical index. This is very useful for locating libraries that stock particular books or periodicals, or for carrying out a subject search. The subject index allows for choice of language and restriction of dates. The catalogues of 20 libraries are accessible, including Oxford, Cambridge, Birmingham, the London School of Economics, Imperial College, Manchester, Trinity College, Warwick, and the School of Advanced Studies.

Dag Hammarskjöld Library (*United Nations*)

http://www.un.org/Depts/dhl/ (214)

In addition to access to the library catalogue, which documents all UN publications held by the library, there is also information on the UN system of documentation, a UN documentation research guide, and information on UN depository libraries.

Gabriel: National Libraries of Europe

http://www.bl.uk/gabriel/en/countries.html (215)

Links to their Home pages.

Law Libraries

http://www2.spfo.unibo.it/spolfo/LIBRARY.htm#lib (216)

A listing from the University of Bologna.

Law Library Catalogs (*USA*)

http://www.washlaw.edu/lawcat/lawcat.html (217)

LIBDEX – Countries (*The Library Index*)

http://www.libdex.com/country.html (218)

A listing of library catalogues that are accessible over the Web, arranged by country, then by type (e.g. academic, business, public). Very useful for establishing whether libraries that are geographically proximate hold the books that you are interested in. Note: libraries in the UK are listed under region (England, Wales, Scotland, Northern Ireland). There are links to the URLs of the catalogues in many instances, as well as to the Home pages of the library service, which will provide information on access and conditions.

LIBWEB Library Servers via WWW

http://sunsite.berkeley.edu/Libweb/ (219)

Lists more than 6000 library pages worldwide. Updated daily.

World Directory Parliamentary Libraries

http://www.bundestag.de/datbk/library/index.html (220)

Provided by the Web service of the German Bundestag. Arranged by country. Once the country is selected, choose the legislative body, which returns a record that provides extensive information under a number of headings relating to its library service. This includes contact information, details of the library (acquisitions budget, staffing, holdings size, periodicals, cuttings availability, number of loans per year, etc.), publications produced by the library, and parliamentary documents produced.

(9) News

(a) General news

Current Awareness Resources via Streaming Audio & Video

http://gwis2.circ.gwu.edu/~gprice/audio.htm (221)

Provided by Gary Price, George Washington University. A large number of links to current news and television broadcasts from the USA, Canada, Britain, Israel, and many other countries. There are also links to schedules for some programmes, and to archived streaming materials. You will need a viewer for these feeds, namely *Real Player*, which is available at no charge from *http://www.real.com/* (222).

News Index

http://www.newsindex.com/ (223)

A search engine that has been around since 1996. It pulls up links to *current* news items from a large database of sources; there are no archived materials here. For instance, on 18 September 2001, the query *Taliban* returned 1158 links.

OnlineNewspapers.com

http://www.onlinenewspapers.com/ (224)

Created and maintained by Web Wombat, this metasite lists some 10,000 online newspapers from around the world, which are arranged by geographical and political entity.

Pandia Newsfinder

http://www.pandia.com/news/index.html (225)

A search engine that taps major newsmedia sources of information, including BBC, CNN, *Washington Post, Financial Times, Guardian,* and *Independent.*

(b) Legal news

Many of the other sections in this law subject directory include references to sites that provide current UK, national, and international legal news. These include 9.1 Associations/institutions, 9.16 Subject areas, 9.17 Subject directories and gateways, and 9.20 UK Government, legal bodies, legislation, and organisations.

International Law Office Newsletters

http://www.internationallawoffice.com/subscribe.cfm (226)

This is a free service that is made available by the *International Law Office,* which provides 'online commentaries as specialist Legal Newsletters. Written in collaboration with over 500 of the world's leading experts and covering more than 80 jurisdictions, it delivers individually requested information via email to an influential global audience of law firm partners and international corporate counsel.' Information is provided that covers 30 subject areas. If you select the *Newsletters* link, you access a search engine that allows you to select the subject area, and are then provided with a list of entries arranged by country for that subject field; if you select the country, you are provided with information in all subject areas that is in the database for that country. If you select the *News* link, which accesses the news archive search engine, you can filter by country, subject field, keyword, and date, the latter from 1997. You can also elect to have specific subject newsletters emailed to you if you subscribe to this service, for which there is no charge.

Law gazette.co.uk

http://www.lawgazette.co.uk/homeframe.asp (227)

The official magazine of The Law Society, England and Wales. In addition to current news items and *job* search, the archive includes materials dating from 1998.

Legal Week

http://www.lwk.co.uk/ (228)

Provides breaking news on legal matters, which is subdivided into a number of different sections: legal week (UK), legal IT, legal week global, legal student, legal jobs, legal director, and legal mall. The archive available online dates back to 1998. You can subscribe to particular sections so that these are emailed to you, for which there is no charge.

NewsNow: Law

http://www.newsnow.co.uk/cgi/NewsNow/NewsNow.htm?Theme=Law (229)

An electronic newswire service providing information on breaking news, divided by time units (1 to 2 hours old, etc.) from across the Web. Essentially this type of service taps into other news databases to extract news on particular subject matters. There is an archive of earlier news, dating back approximately one month. If you need to be kept up to date on legal news worldwide as soon as it breaks, this service will probably fit the bill.

The Lawyer.com

http://www.interactive-lawyer.com/ (230)

Current legal news, worldwide. The archive carries some 25,000 articles, dating from 1996. However, when the site was explored last, they were experiencing technical difficulties with this (24 August 2002). To access the archive select *Lawyer News* and then *Lawyer Library*.

Web Journal of Current Legal Issues

http://webjcli.ncl.ac.uk/ (231)

Published by the University of Newcastle upon Tyne, it 'is published bi-monthly. . . . The focus of the Journal is on current legal issues in judicial decisions, law reform, legislation, legal research, policy related socio-legal research, legal information, information technology and practice.' Archived issues dating back to 1995 are available.

(10) Reference gateways

Martindale's: The Reference Desk

http://www-sci.lib.uci.edu/HSG/Ref.html (232)

(11) Travel

(*Air*) Airline Network

http://www.airline-network.co.uk/Homepage/Homepage.asp (233)

(*Air*) cheapflights.com

http://www.cheapflights.com/ (234)

(*Air*) Dial A Flight

http://www.dialaflight.com/ (235)

(*Air*) Mile Marker: Online Air Distance Calculator

http://www.webflyer.com/milemarker/milemarker.htm (236)

(*Bus*) UK Bus Timetable Website Directory

http://www.showbus.co.uk/timetables/index.html (237)

(*Coach*) GoByCoach.com

http://www.gobycoach.com/gbchome.cfm?from=www.nationalexpress.co.uk (238)

Includes National Express coaches, Eurolines, and JetLink.

EmbassyWorld.Com

http://www.embassyworld.com/ (239)

The search engine available here allows you to access the Home pages of the embassy of a country located in a specified other country. You can also access the visa requirements of a particular country.

(*Rail*) European National Timetables and Railways

http://mercurio.iet.unipi.it/misc/timetabl.html (240)

Links to Home pages of national railways, online timetables, and planners.

(*Rail*) Timetables Online

http://www.rail.co.uk/ukrail/planner/planner.htm (241)

FXConverter (*Foreign Exchange Currency Converter*)

http://www.oanda.com/convert/classic (242)

World Clock-Time Zones

http://www.timeanddate.com/worldclock/ (243)

xe.com The Universal Currency Converter

http://www.xe.com/ucc/ (244)

(12) Universities and colleges

American Universities

http://www.clas.ufl.edu/CLAS/american-universities.html (245)

Links to the Home pages of US institutions of higher education offering Bachelor degrees and higher.

Braintrack University Index

http://www.braintrack.com/ (246)

Links to 5500 institutions of higher education in 161 countries (September 2001).

Canadian Universities

http://www.uwaterloo.ca/canu/ (247)

Links to Home pages.

UK Universities and Colleges (*Alphabetical Listing*)

http://www.scit.wlv.ac.uk/ukinfo/alpha.html (248)

Universities and Colleges Admissions Service for the UK

http://www.ucas.ac.uk/ (249)

Information for students on courses available at UK institutions of higher education, on application procedures, etc.

Universities and HE Colleges

http://bubl.ac.uk/uk/he.htm (250)

Includes links arranged by UK, worldwide, and USA. There are also links to UK Research Councils, and various higher education administrative organisations, such as the DFEE, HEFCE, QAA, and UCAS.

Universities Worldwide

http://geowww.uibk.ac.at/univ/ (251)

Links to some 6265 universities in 170 countries. Separate listing for US universities.

University of Wolverhampton UK Sensitive Maps

http://www.scit.wlv.ac.uk/ukinfo/uk.map.html (252)

A geographical image map of UK Universities and Higher Education Colleges, which is associated with a topic index. By default the topic index is set to *Home page* so that when you select the institution from the map, the link directs you there. Other categories include: research, alumni, RAE and QAA assessments, and admissions. There is also an image map of research sites and a series of maps are being developed for institutions of further education. Until the latter are completed, a listing is available.

9.15 Research and funding

CORDIS

http://www.cordis.lu (253)

CORDIS is the (European) Community Research and Development Information Service of the European Commission, providing information on EU research and exploitation possibilities.

Economic and Social Research Council

http://www.esrc.ac.uk/home.html (254)

The ESRC is the largest and main funding agency in the UK for research and postgraduate training in the social and economic sciences. Detailed information is provided on the grants available under various headings, including amounts and submission deadlines. Latest News Reports and the Social Science Newsletter provide information on recent activities and projects.

Getting Funded

http://www.hero.ac.uk/research/getting_funded226.cfm (255)

A listing of UK-based sources of funding from *HERO*, see above, *General*.

Guide to European Funding Opportunities for UK Social Science

http://www.lboro.ac.uk/departments/eu/esrclh.html (256)

Detailed information is provided in the form of Information Sheets relating to funding opportunities available for social scientific research and social scientists, primarily through the European Commission. There is a general introduction and information on fund provision through different Commission frameworks (FPIV and FPV), as well as on specific programmes. The latter include Targeted Socio-Economic Research (TSER), Training and Mobility of Researchers (TMR), European Co-operation in the field of Scientific and Technical Research (COST), and DG Discretionary Funds.

Joseph Rowntree Charitable Trust

http://www.jrct.org.uk/ (257)

Leverhulme Trust

http://www.leverhulme.org.uk/index.html (258)

Lotto *(National Lottery) Community Fund*

http://www.nlcb.org.uk (259)

Regard

http://www.regard.ac.uk/regard/home/index_html (260)

'Searchable database which is a key source of information on ESRC-funded research. Information is available on initial projects, the research results, and resulting publications and outputs. Outputs include books, journal and newspaper articles, conference papers, media broadcasts and software. Links to research project Web sites and online publications are provided where available. Contains over 70,000 records covering research from 1984 to the present and is updated daily.' The database can be searched by keyword, name of researcher, and ESRC reference number. Available also is information on ESRC research centres, including links to their Home pages. Records explored can be collated for batch printing.

The Foundation Center

http://fdncenter.org (261)

The Foundation is a US-based organisation that is 'an independent nonprofit information clearinghouse established in 1956. The Center's mission is to foster public understanding of the foundation field by collecting, organizing, analyzing, and disseminating information on foundations, corporate giving, and related subjects. The audiences that call on the Center's resources include grantseekers, grantmakers, researchers, policymakers, the media, and the general public.'

UK Fundraising

http://www.fundraising.co.uk/ (262)

This site has a wealth of information relating to all aspects of fundraising. Although its primary focus is not that of raising funds for scholarly research or the financing of education courses, there is relevant information on these as well. There are separate sections on Education, and on Grants and Funding.

9.16 Subject areas

See also 9.2 Case law/legislation, 9.6 Legal research, and 9.19 Treaties and international agreements.

(1) Asylum and immigration law

asylumlaw.org

http://www.asylumlaw.org/ (263)

Information, worldwide, relating to immigration, refugee status, and asylum. In addition to breaking news items, of particular interest is the *SUPER Search* engine and the HRDE database. Super Search is a meta-search engine that queries 14 human rights databases simultaneously. They include Amnesty International, the Canadian Immigration and Refugee Board, and the Australian Refugee Tribunal. The latter database includes more than 20,000 decisions. Before use it is worth reading the *About* information.

HRDE is the acronym for Human Rights Documents Exchange, which was a Texas-based organisation that compiled reports on various human rights issues, including asylum and refugee status, and collated reports compiled by other organisations, including the US Department of State, the Home Office, and the UNHCR (UN High Commissioner for Refugees). There are some 895 reports in the database, in PDF format. There is no search engine, but those dealing more specifically with asylum related matters are listed from page 18. Earlier pages list reports dealing with persecution in various countries and violations of human rights.

Asylum Support

http://www.asylumsupport.info/ (264)

Site managed by Frank Corrigan. The site includes links to resources on many issues relating to migration and asylum. *Bill and White Paper* links to resources that include the full text of the Nationality, Immigration and Asylum Bill, background information thereto, the white paper, *Secure Borders, Safe Haven*, and a list of advocacy groups. *Publications* links to a very lengthy list of document resources, many of which are directly relevant to asylum-migration issues as currently debated in the UK.

CISNEWS

http://www.cis.org/mail_login.html (265)

This is the URL to subscribe to the mailing list provided by the Center for Immigration Studies, a Washington, DC, based non-profit research organisation. The mailing list, which has some 5000 subscribers, provides information on immigration news from around the world, in the form of two postings a day, one dealing with the USA, and the other non-US territories. The Center, *http://www.cis.org/* (266), also publishes various reports.

Country Assessments – April 2002

http://www.ind.homeoffice.gov.uk/default.asp?pageid=88 (267)

Produced by the Country Information and Policy Unit of the Home Office Appeals and Policy Directorate, these reports are assessments of those countries that are the source of the largest numbers of asylum applications in the UK. 'The purpose of these country assessments is to inform decision-making on asylum applications by Home Office caseworkers and to assist other officials involved in the asylum determination process.'

Electronic Immigration Network (*EIN*)

http://www.ein.org.uk/ (268)

The EIN is a voluntary organisation with charitable status. The resource is divided into two components: a database of links that is accessible without charge, and a case law database for which there is a subscription charge. The links cover a wide spectrum that goes beyond the confines of immigration and asylum law in the strict sense, but is, nonetheless, very comprehensive, covering immigration law and asylum issues in the UK, Europe, and worldwide.

European Council on Refugees and Exiles

http://www.ecre.org/ (269)

'ECRE is an umbrella organisation of 73 refugee-assisting agencies in 30 countries working towards fair and humane policies for the treatment of asylum seekers and refugees.' Current news, documents relating to European policies, responses to proposals, and reports.

Guide to International Refugee Law Resources on the Web

http://www.llrx.com/features/refugee.htm (270)

Compiled by Elisa Mason, who worked for six years with the UNHCR, published July 2000.

Refugee Case Law Site

http://www.refugeecaselaw.org/Refugee/Default.asp (271)

Provided by the University of Michigan Law School. 'The site currently collects, indexes, and publishes selected recent court decisions that interpret the legal definition of a "refugee." It presently contains cases from the highest national courts of Australia, Austria, Canada, Germany, New Zealand, Switzerland, the United Kingdom, and the United States.' Also available are the Home Office Country Assessments.

(2) Commercial law

Cyberbanking and Law

http://rechtsinformatik.jura.uni-sb.de/cbl/ (272)

Statutes and decisions arranged by country, papers, and resources on security issues. As this is a German site, a significant number of resources are in that language.

E-Commerce Law Resources

http://www.bmck.com/ecommerce/home-transactions.htm (273)

Many of the resources are of primary relevance to US lawyers. There is, however, a section on legislation, regulations and policies by country, for e-commerce, privacy, and information security law.

E-Commerce Times

http://www.ecommercetimes.com/ (274)

Online news sheet devoted to coverage of e-commerce issues.

European Union: Competition

http://europa.eu.int/comm/competition/index_en.html (275)

Official EU Commission site with latest news, proposals, case law, legislation, and other documents relating to antitrust, mergers, liberalisation, and state aid.

Law and E-Commerce

http://europa.eu.int/information_society/topics/ebusiness/ecommerce/ 8epolicy_elaw/law_ecommerce/index_en.htm (276)

EU site that collates information relating to law and e-commerce under a large number of headings, including applicable law/jurisdiction, cybercrime, distance selling, digital signatures, electronic contracts, international treaties and conventions, intellectual property rights (IPR), payments, and privacy.

Lex Mercatoria

http://www.lexmercatoria.org/ (277)

This site, provided by Cameron May, international law publishers, collates access to a significant volume of resources classified under: international economic law, international tax and financial regulation, international commercial arbitration, international trade law, private international commercial law, carriage, transport and maritime law, intellectual property, and electronic commerce and encryption, and others. The site provides access to various conventions, and laws and regulations relating to these matters.

(3) Constitutional law

Constitution Finder

http://confinder.richmond.edu/ (278)

Produced at the School of Law, University of Richmond, links arranged by country to their constitutions, and information thereon.

Political Database of the Americas

http://www.georgetown.edu/pdba/english.html (279)

Access to constitutions of the countries of the Organization of American States (OAS) and Cuba in the original languages of their composition.

Researching Constitutional Law on the Internet

http://www.lib.uchicago.edu/~llou/conlaw.html (280)

Provided by the Library of the University of Chicago.

(4) Employment law

Employment Law Super Portal

http://www.emplaw.co.uk/topinfo/portal.htm (281)

See the link to *Key Employment Law Sites*. Resources available here include case law, which consists of employment cases that have been filtered from various courts (e.g. House of Lords, Court of Appeal, European Court of Human Rights), main employment statutes, statutory instruments, EC/EU materials, current employment-related bills, official guidance on various categories of employment related issues, and trade union employment matters.

Natlex

http://natlex.ilo.org/scripts/natlexcgi.exe?lang=E (282)

Provided by the International Labour Organization, a bibliographic database of national laws on labour, social security, and related rights. The database has some 61,000 entries that are ordered by country/subjects and subjects/countries, and date of text.

(5) Environmental law

ECOLEX: A Gateway to Environmental Law

http://www.ecolex.org/ (283)

A joint project between the UNEP (United Nations Environmental Programme), IUCN (World Conservation Union), and the FAO (UN Food and Agricultural Organization), it provides databases of multilateral treaties, international soft law and related documents, instruments of the European union, national legislation, court decisions and law and policy literature. The databases can be searched by a range of fields.

European Environmental Law Homepage

http://www.eel.nl/ (284)

A substantial volume of resources are accessible at this site, including treaties, legislation, case law, documents, dossiers, breaking news, and information on conferences. There is also a European environmental law database that contains most cases decided by the European Court of Justice and the Court of First Instance, which can be searched on a number of fields, including case no, parties, sector, and decision date. By leaving the fields empty and selecting the *Search* button, the cases are listed in reverse chronological order.

International Environmental Law Research Guide

http://www.ll.georgetown.edu/intl/guides/environment/ (285)

Prepared by Georgetown University law library. Sections include bibliographies and research guides, background and general sources, treaties, national and international statutes, and national and international case law.

IUCN: Environmental Law Programme

http://www.iucn.org/themes/law/ (286)

The World Conservation Union was founded in 1948, to bring together states, government agencies, and NGOs, in the cause of 'conserving the integrity and diversity of nature and to ensure that any use of natural resources is equitable and ecologically sustainable.' There are some 980 members in 140 countries. The site provides information on the current work of its Environmental Law Commission and Environmental Law Centre, its current advocacy, and publications, the most recent of which are available online.

United Nations Environmental Programme (*UNEP*)

http://www.unep.org/ (287)

News, links to conventions, information by regions on environmental issues and programmes, links to agencies involved in environmental programmes, information and resources relating to international conferences. The focus areas provide news on specific topics (e.g. atmosphere, energy, sustainable consumption). An essential resource for monitoring environmental issues at the international level.

(6) Human rights/humanitarian law

Amnesty International

http://www.amnesty.org/ (288)

Current news, campaigns, commentary, reports.

Civilrights.org (*US*)

http://www.civilrights.org/ (289)

This site has a mass of information relating to a variety of civil rights issues. The categories include affirmative action, civil rights enforcement, disability, hate crimes, immigration, indigenous issues, poverty/welfare, and social security/senior issues. The archive includes news articles, reports, position papers, essays, and government documents.

Derechos

http://www.derechos.org/ (290)

Derechos means rights in Spanish. This site provides excellent resources on human rights, arranged by region.

For the Record 2001: The European Human Rights System

http://www.hri.ca/fortherecord2001/euro2001/index.htm (291)

Produced by the Netherlands Institute of Human Rights since 2000, in structure it parallels the report *For the Record: The United Nations Human Rights System; see* below. Divided into two volumes, the first provides information on its mechanisms and legal framework, the second a country-by-country analysis. Unlike the UN version, it provides a summary of case law in the context of the country profiles. This is a useful resource, although the information provided is somewhat less detailed than that provided by its sister publication.

For the Record 2001: The United Nations Human Rights System

http://www.hri.ca/fortherecord2001/index.htm (292)

Produced by Human Rights Internet, this resource provides systematically presented information relating to the system of human rights administered by the UN, its performance, and its implementation and observance by member states. Although the above URL references the report for 2001, reports are available beginning in 1997, in French as well as English.

Volume 1 provides information on thematic mechanisms and approaches, which outline the workings of the UN human rights system and its constituent officers and bodies. It also provides a glossary, a chapter dealing with methodological and technical issues, one on special mechanisms of the Commission of Human Rights, and a schedule of current and forthcoming reports. Where applicable, the chapter on thematic mechanisms provides access to the reports of the Special Rapporteurs, and there is also information on developments under a variety of headings.

The other volumes provide information on human rights in particular countries and territories, arranged by region. This includes information on their treaty and ratification status, their reports to treaty bodies, and thematic reports. There are cross-referenced hyperlinks to many reports.

This is a very useful resource for monitoring the status of human rights in particular countries, as well as for accessing information on the complex UN system of human rights implementation and monitoring.

Freedom in the World 1999–2000

http://www.freedomhouse.org/research/freeworld/2000/countries.htm (293)

Published by Freedom House, an American-based non-profit organisation, it is an annual review of the progress/retreat of civil and political liberties in particular countries. In this edition 192 countries are covered. In addition to information relating directly to civil and political liberties, each report includes information on demographics, purchasing power parities, life expectancy, ethnic groups, and capital. Detailed information is provided on the methodology of the survey.

Human Rights Brief

http://www.wcl.american.edu/hrbrief/issue.cfm (294)

An online journal published by the Washington College of Law, dealing with human rights law, both in the USA and internationally. There are three issues a year, and nine volumes can be accessed online.

Human Rights Library

http://www1.umn.edu/humanrts/ (295)

Provided by the University of Minnesota, the section on *Human Rights Documents and Materials* has links to some 10,400 documents, including treaties and other international instruments, regional materials, bibliographies, and refugee and asylum resources, and links to thousands of related sites. One of the top human rights sites.

Human Rights Unit

http://www.lcd.gov.uk/hract/ (296)

A division of the Lord Chancellor's department charged with overseeing the implementation of the Human Rights Act 1998. Includes text of the act, an archive on Human Rights Act proceedings through the legislature, the rights under the convention, as listed in Schedule 1, commencement and amendment orders, reviews of human rights instruments, and links to other human rights instruments.

Human Rights Watch

http://www.hrw.org/ (297)

Current news, campaigns, commentary, reports.

International Commission of Jurists

http://www.icj.org/ (298)

Site provides access to fact-finding mission reports, documents, trial observation reports, and publications.

Internet Law Library Civil Liberties and Civil Rights: General

http://www.lawguru.com/ilawlib/93.htm (299)

Links to international and national legislation on civil liberties and human rights. See also the links at the top of the page to legislation relating to gender, indigenous peoples, and religion and government.

Liberty (*UK*)

http://www.liberty-human-rights.org.uk/ (300)

Web site of the UK pressure group concerned with issues of civil rights, which 'works to promote human rights and protect civil liberties through a combination of test case litigation, lobbying, campaigning and research'. The site includes pages that address topical issues and the response of the organisation to them, including legal opinions by barristers. The materials are arranged in an alphabetical index and there is no search engine.

United Nations High Commissioner for Human Rights

http://www.unhchr.ch/ (301)

Main portal for resources on the UN system of human rights. The system is quite complex so a good starting point is the Index. See also *United Nations System* (organisational chart), at *http://www.un.org/aboutun/chart.html* (302).

War and Peace

http://www.law.ecel.uwa.edu.au/intlaw/war_and_peace.htm (303)

Provided by Professor Francis Auburn, University of Western Australia.

War Crime Material

http://www.nesl.edu/research/warcrim.cfm (304)

Provided by New York University School of Law, primary materials, articles online, international criminal tribunals, and research guides.

Web Genocide Documentation Centre

http://www.ess.uwe.ac.uk/genocide.htm (305)

Primary materials on war crimes and genocide: World War II, former Yugoslavia, Kosovo, East Timor, and others.

(7) Intellectual property

European Union: Intellectual Property

http://europa.eu.int/scadplus/leg/en/s06020.htm (306)

Information on EU objectives, regulations, and policies concerning intellectual property.

Intellectual Property Law

http://www.intelproplaw.com/ (307)

'The intellectual property law server provides information about intellectual property law including patent, trademark and copyright. Resources include comprehensive links, general information, space for professionals to publish articles and forums for discussing related issues.' The *News Matrix* search engine links to latest news from a number of sources (Yahoo News Headlines, Lycos, News.com, Tech Web, ZDNet News, and Dogpile) on intellectual property, patents, copyright, trade marks, and trade secrets. There is also a large archive of articles relating to these subjects. US and international in orientation.

Intellectual Property Legislation arranged by country

See 9.2 Case law/legislation, **CLEA**.

IP Web Resources

http://www.ipmall.fplc.edu/web_resources/fplchome.htm (308)

Although this list from Pierce Law's IP Mall focuses principally on US-related law and issues, there are some useful resources that fall outside these limits.

Patent Office: UK

http://www.patent.gov.uk/ (309)

Information about the Patent Office and its policies, and about trade marks, copyright, designs, and patents. Overview information about trade marks, etc., including history, law, with access to legal decisions, which date from 1998.

TRIPS (Trade-Related aspects of Intellectual Property rights) on the WTO (World Trade Organization) Web site

http://www.wto.org/english/tratop_e/trips_e/trips_e.htm (310)

Various documents clarifying aspects of the agreement.

United States Patent and Trademark Office

http://www.uspto.gov/ (311)

Among the other resources there are databases of US patents and trade marks.

WIPO (*World Intellectual Property Organization*)

http://www.wipo.int/ (312)

WIPO is a specialised agency of the UN and is responsible currently for monitoring and administering 23 international treaties dealing with intellectual property matters, the full texts of which can be accessed from this site.

(8) International law

American Society of International Law: Guide to Electronic Resources for International Law

http://www.asil.org/resource/home.htm (313)

A large collection of detailed annotated links. The main headings under which they are grouped include human rights, international commercial arbitration, international criminal law, international economic law, international environmental law, and private international law. Includes information on research strategies, library materials, bibliographies, periodical literature, and similar.

InternationalADR (*International Alternative Dispute Resolution*)

http://www.internationaladr.com/ (314)

Published by Kluwer Law International in affiliation with the Permanent Court of Arbitration and the Institute for Transnational Arbitration. Links to conventions, model clauses, rules, case law, commentary, institutions, news, and a country index. The latter provides links to relevant legislation and the case law of particular countries.

International Law

http://www.un.org/law/ (315)

A UN Web site. Provides access to UN international law organs, such as the Sixth Committee of the United Nations, the International Criminal Court, the International Court of Justice, and the International Criminal Tribunals. The Documents Research Guide provides introductory information on these bodies with some relevant amplifying links.

International Law Commission

http://www.un.org/law/ilc/index.htm (316)

The Commission is concerned with the codification of international law. Resources that are available include a brief historical overview on international codification and its sources, draft conventions and texts that the Commission, since 1947, has been engaged on, session reports (available online, dated 1996–), information on membership, and various reports.

Permanent Court of Arbitration

http://www.pca-cpa.org/ (317)

Basic documents, recent and pending cases, research and publications, news.

Public International Law

http://www.law.ecel.uwa.edu.au/intlaw/ (318)

Provided by Professor Francis Auburn, University of Western Australia, some 900 links to resources under a wide variety of headings.

(9) Jurisprudence

Jurisprudence

http://mishpat.net/law/Jurisprudence/ (319)

Part of Mishpat.Net's Internet Legal Information site. The categories referenced include critical legal studies, feminist jurisprudence, legal history, legal positivism and realism, and religious law. The number of links referenced in each is relatively small.

(10) Law and information technology

Bytes in Brief

http://www.senseient.com/bytesinbrief/bytes.asp?page=currentbytes (320)

A monthly digest of news on Internet law and technology news, which can be viewed online, or which can be subscribed to for delivery by electronic mail, at *http://www.senseient.com/bytesinbrief/subscribe.asp* (321), for which there is no charge. The archive, at *http://www.senseient.com/bytesinbrief/archive.asp* (322), dates back to July 1997.

Cyber-Crime

http://www.privacyinternational.org/issues/cybercrime/index.html (323)

Part of *Privacy International*, this site collates a large volume of resources dealing with issues of electronic freedom, cyber crime, and controls, and is international in focus. In addition to an extensive list of *News*, it includes documents, country surveys, and links to other resources.

Cyber-Rights and Cyber-Liberties

http://www.cyber-rights.org/ (324)

UK-based civil liberties organisation that campaigns for freedom of speech and privacy on the Internet. The resources available monitor EU, international, and UK attempts to regulate activities via the Internet, whether this is crime, dissemination of racial hatred, security, or privacy, inasmuch as such regulation is likely to impinge on individual freedoms and privacy. The resource provides access to information relating to ongoing regulatory activities, reports, and links to some published materials that are available online. The site is not very well organised in terms of navigation, so scroll down to the bottom of the page for some additional links.

Electronic Frontier Foundation

http://www.eff.org/ (325)

Veteran US organisation 'working to protect our fundamental rights regardless of technology; to educate the press, policymakers and the general public about civil liberties issues related to technology; and to act as a defender of those liberties. Among our various activities, EFF opposes misguided legislation, initiates and defends court cases preserving individuals' rights, launches global public campaigns, introduces leading edge proposals and papers, hosts frequent educational events, engages the press regularly, and publishes a comprehensive archive of digital civil liberties information at one of the most linked-to websites in the world.' There is a large volume of resources at this site relating to free speech online, audiovisual freedom, copyright issues, and online freedoms, which the organisation campaigns about vigorously. While it is particularly concerned with the impact of these matters in the USA, it highlights similar concerns in other countries.

Electronic Privacy Information Center

http://epic.org/ (326)

The site includes current news items relating to electronic privacy, cryptography, freedom of information, and free speech, and an archive of such items dating back to 1998, which are linked to relevant documents and resources.

Global Internet Liberty Campaign

http://www.gilc.org/ (327)

The GILC is a coalition of groups such as the American Civil Liberties Union, Human Rights Watch, Liberty, and many other human rights organisations worldwide. The major issues that GILC collates resources and reports about are free speech, privacy, cryptography, and access to electronic communications.

International Journal of Law and Information Technology

http://www3.oup.co.uk/inttec/contents/ (328)

Published by Oxford University Press, an online journal whose online texts date from 1996. The journal focuses on computer law and the application of computer technology to legal practice.

Legal Technology Insider

http://www.legaltechnology.org/ (329)

Electronic newsletter with UK focus with archives dating back to January 2001.

(11) Personal injury

Brain and Spine Injury

http://www.exchangechambers.co.uk/billbraithwaite/ (330)

The Web site of Bill Braithwaite, Barrister QC, who specialises in brain and spinal injury cases. It includes a significant number of articles, case reports, and case settlement reports. These are well written and likely to be informative for those involved in these types of personal injury cases. The *Jokes* page is likely to be better appreciated after having consulted his *Fees* page.

(12) Roman law

Roman Law Resources

http://iuscivile.com/ (331)

The site is maintained by Professor Ernest Metzger, University of Aberdeen, and provides access to a significant volume of materials relating to Roman law. This includes bibliographies, secondary literature online, online primary sources on Roman and civil law and related subjects, some compilations of laws and rescripts, a directory of teachers of Roman law in various countries, a directory of journals devoted to Roman and civil law and related subjects, lists of antiquarian booksellers, etc. This site is probably the best place to start looking for online Roman law resources.

9.17 Subject directories and gateways

(1) Law

Chan Robles Virtual Law Library

http://www.chanrobles.com/topic.htm (332)

Although this subject directory is smaller than most of those referenced below, it is quite well focused and has links to some useful resources.

FindLaw

http://www.findlaw.com/ (333)

This US-based law subject directory includes links to masses of information, classified under four main categories relating to targeted audiences: legal professionals, students, business, and public. The division between the first two can usefully be ignored as far as the student is concerned. Main sub-divisions under *legal professionals* include: legal subjects, laws (cases and codes), foreign and international, legal organisations, software and technology, continuing legal education, and legal careers. In the *students* section there are main entries for law schools, law reviews, law student resources, employment, and the bar.

Hieros Gamos

http://www.hg.org/ (334)

One of the largest general law subject directories, American based. Major divisions include US law, international law, legal associations, bar associations, law practice center, student law center, and law library and news center. There are thousands of links to resources relating to virtually every aspect and type of law, from legislation to enforcement. The site lacks a search engine, and in many cases the postal addresses of firms and associations, particularly non-US, are given rather than hyperlinks to Home pages, even when these are available. However, you can always copy the name of the organisation/firm/body and paste as a query into Google, or the Google toolbar if you have this installed.

Infolaw

http://www.infolaw.co.uk/ (335)

Lengthy lists of largely non-annotated links to subject specialisms and other law related resources. The *Law Resources* link focuses on UK and associated European/EU law-related sites. There is also an *Overseas Law Resources* section.

Jurist UK

http://jurist.law.cam.ac.uk/ (336)

The UK site of the better known US site, *http://jurist.law.pitt.edu/* (337). The main headings under which resources are arranged are: studying law, UK legal news, UK legal research, world law, teaching law, and legal scholarship.

Law and Politics Internet Guide

http://www.lpig.org/ (338)

A useful annotated subject directory with a US bias as far as resources/law is concerned. The inclusion of *Politics* in the title is somewhat misleading as nearly all the section entries relate to law/legal issues.

Lawlinks: Legal Information on the Internet

http://library.ukc.ac.uk/library/lawlinks/ (339)

Developed by Sarah Carter, librarian, University of Kent, Canterbury. Main sections include: gateways and portals, UK resources, European Union, international law, human rights, and private international law. This directory does not, however, always note when resources linked to are available only by subscription.

Legal Resources in the UK and Ireland, Maintained by Delia Venables

http://www.venables.co.uk/ (340)

Divided into four sections: information for individuals, for lawyers, for companies, and for students.

Mishpat.Net Internet Legal Information

http://mishpat.net/ (341)

Categories include cyberlaw, criminal law, labor law, intellectual property, legal procedure, and family law. A relatively small, clearly presented, and manageable law subject directory. US in focus.

Scottish Law Online

http://www.scottishlaw.org.uk/ (342)

Information on Scottish law, legal procedures, and organisations.

WWW Virtual Library – Law

http://www.law.indiana.edu/v-lib/ (343)

Maintained by the Indiana University School of Law, Bloomington. The resources can be searched by keyword, by topical listing, and by information source.

(2) Social sciences and general

The subject directories listed below include sections specifically on law, and/ or resources on other subjects likely to be of interest to law students and practitioners, covering, as they do, a wide range of subject matter.

BUBL (*Bulletin Board for Libraries*)

http://www.bubl.ac.uk (344)

Originally funded by the Joint Information Systems Committee of the Higher Education Funding Councils for England, Wales and Scotland, this is a subject gateway to high-quality resources considered to be of interest to students and staff in higher education, including, but not confined to, those in the social sciences. Although the subject areas covered are extensive, the number of resources listed for each one is relatively small in comparison with some other directories.

dmoz Open Directory Project

http://dmoz.org/ (345)

This site purports to be the largest subject directory on the Web, including more than 2.9 million annotated links. In structure it is similar to Yahoo, albeit larger, but it does not take any advertising and is edited by more than 42,000 volunteer editors. The *Society* category, which subsumes sociology, social science, politics, psychology, law, government, and others, includes some 228,650 links, 19,706 in the category law (28 August 2002).

Infomine: Scholarly Internet Resource Collection

http://infomine.ucr.edu/ (346)

Links to 20,000+ 'academically valuable resources', in various subject fields, but including social sciences and humanities, which in this database subsumes law. Provided by the Library, University of California, Riverside, this is an US equivalent to the UK BUBL or SOSIG resource. The links are annotated. Although these can be browsed alphabetically, in most cases it will be speedier and less taxing to use the search engine. Choose the advanced option so that you can filter by subject and other variables.

JISC Resource Guide for the Social Sciences

http://www.jisc.ac.uk/subject/socsci/ (347)

JISC is the Joint Information Services Committee, which is funded by the UK Higher Education Councils. This file provides details on a 'range of resources [that have] been set up specifically to meet the needs of those working and studying in the social sciences'. The resources available include bibliographic, reference, and research information (e.g. International Bibliography of the Social Sciences), Publications Online, this being databases of full text publications (e.g. PCI Full Text, which comprises indexes of social science and humanities journals between 1770 and 1990), links to subject gateways (e.g. SOSIG, see entry below), and various datasets.

As far as availability is concerned, there are three categories. *Subscription required* means that the resource is available to subscribing institutions of higher education. *Conditionally available* means the resource is available online to all institutions of higher education, although you may require a password, obtainable through higher education institutions. *Freely available* indicates that the resource is available to all accessing it.

Social Sciences Virtual Library

http://www.clas.ufl.edu/users/gthursby/socsci/ (348)

A large collection of carefully reviewed annotated links, including directories and data archives, social science electronic journals, WWW resources by subject, and WWW resources arranged alphabetically.

SOSIG (*Social Science Information Gateway*)

http://www.sosig.ac.uk/ (349)

A subject gateway that is funded by the UK Joint Information Systems Committee and the Economic and Social Research Council. Entries are annotated and can be accessed by using the search engine, or from the subject directories, which include those for economics, law, philosophy, psychology, social welfare, sociology, and women's studies. The *Law* section is divided into general law, UK law, EU law, other jurisdictions law, international law, and law by subject matter.

World Wide Web Virtual Library Central Database

http://conbio.net/vl/database/output.cfm (350)

The World Wide Web Virtual Library is a collection of resources arranged by subject matter compiled by experts in the field. Generally, the resources linked to are of a high quality, have been checked by the subject specialist compiler, and are updated on a regular basis. As gateways to subject-specific resources these are generally far superior to subject directories such as Yahoo. Sites that are included in this network are governed by general rules relating to the quality and organisation of the resources that are listed, which are reviewed by a committee selected from among those who are involved in their compilation.

Yahoo

http://uk.yahoo.com/ (351) *(UK) http://www.yahoo.com/ (main site)* (352)

If you use the UK-based site, you can elect to search either for files on UK servers, or those worldwide. However, the identification of country codes from URLs is problematic so that you may find many links to files on servers outside the UK, even if you choose to initiate your search from the UK site, and check the UK only box.

9.18 Technology

ABA Legal Technology Resource Center

http://www.abanet.org/tech/ltrc/home.html (353)

Provided by the American Bar Association, articles and resources dealing with the provision of legal services and IT technology, including articles, software resources, software comparisons, hardware, Internet technologies, Web development and e-commerce, court technology, and technology and ethics.

9.19 Treaties and international agreements

Environmental Treaties and Resource Indicators (*ENTRI*)

http://sedac.ciesin.org/pidb/pidb-home.html (354)

This very useful resource is provided by a number of cooperating institutions, including Columbia University and NASA, which is worth using as a first port of call for matters relating to environmental treaties. In addition to providing access to the full texts of environmental treaties, the resource provides information about resource problems that the treaties are directed at tackling, and on 'issues that arise at the intersection between global environmental change and the international political and legal system.'

An easy starting point is the *ENTRI Table of Contents*. This provides access to a Free Text Search of the treaties, a chronological, subject, and alphabetical listing of treaties, as well as a chronological and alphabetical listing of treaty summaries. There is also access to tables that provide information on when treaties entered into force, which treaties are in force for a given state, and which states are party to a given treaty. From these there are links to the treaties themselves. The thematic guide to using the resource should be consulted.

Foreign and Commonwealth Office: Treaties

http://www.fco.gov.uk/servlet/Front?pagename=OpenMarket/Xcelerate/ ShowPage&c=Page&cid=1007029396014 (355)

This section of the FCO Web site provides information relating to the conclusion and ratification of international treaties (e.g. the Ponsonby Rule, MOUs), a short glossary of terms relating to international treaties, and access to the full texts of multilateral treaties for which the Government of the United Kingdom is a depositary.

Intellectual Property Treaties

http://www.wipo.int/treaties/index.html (356)

Full text and information concerning ratifications, published by WIPO, the World Intellectual Property Organization, a specialised agency of the UN.

International Humanitarian Law

http://www.icrc.org/ihl (357)

Full text of treaties provided by the International Committee of the Red Cross. See also ***http://www.icrc.org/Web/eng/siteeng0.nsf/iwpList2 Humanitarian_law*** (358) which provides access to information on particular topics and current issues.

List of Treaties and Other International Agreements of the United States in Force

http://www.state.gov/s/l/c3431.htm (359)

The files are in PDF format; right click and save to disk, then open in PDF viewer, unless you have a browser with an Adobe reader plugin.

Multilaterals Project

http://fletcher.tufts.edu/multilaterals.html (360)

An ongoing project at the Fletcher School of Law & Diplomacy, Tufts University, Medford, Massachusetts, to make accessible international multilateral conventions and other instruments. These are grouped under atmosphere and space, cultural protection, general, marine and coastal, trade and commercial relations, flora and fauna biodiversity, diplomatic relations, other environmental, rules of warfare, and arms control. One of the oldest and most respected Internet treaty sources.

Treaties and International Agreements by Subject

http://www.worldlii.org/catalog/2356.html (361)

Provided by the World Legal Information Institute.

United Nations Treaty Collection

http://untreaty.un.org/English/treaty.asp (362)

Under Article 102 of the Charter of the United Nations, 'Every treaty and every international agreement entered into by any Member of the United Nations after the present Charter comes into force shall as soon as possible be registered with the Secretariat and published by it'. Access to the treaty database is by subscription. A printed version is published annually by the UN.

9.20 UK Government, legal bodies, legislation, and organisations

Acts of the UK Parliament

http://www.legislation.hmso.gov.uk/acts.htm (363)

Online access to all Public and Local Acts of the UK Parliament since 1988 and 1991 respectively.

Attorney General's Chambers

http://www.lslo.gov.uk/ (364)

Chronological Tables of Local and Private Acts

http://www.legislation.hmso.gov.uk/ (365)

Tables cover Public Acts passed since 1797, and Local Acts since 1539.

Companies House

http://www.companies-house.gov.uk/ (366)

The search engine allows searches of companies by name, and of directors that have been disqualified.

Criminal Cases Reviews Commission

http://www.ccrc.gov.uk/ (367)

Application form and annual reports.

Criminal Justice System (*England and Wales*)

http://www.cjsonline.org/home.html (368)

Schematic information for consumers and those working within the CJS, providing introductory information with some links on varied components. Also, the CJS annual report, and the Criminal Justice Business Quarterly Report.

Crown Prosecution Service (*England and Wales*)

http://www.cps.gov.uk/ (369)

Daily List

http://www.tso.co.uk/bookshop/bookstore.asp?FO=38793 (370)

A listing of official government publications issued on the day. Users can view the whole list, or by category (e.g. statutory instruments, Scottish acts).

Equal Opportunities Commission

http://www.eoc.org.uk/ (371)

Hansard (*House of Commons Daily Debates*)

http://www.parliament.the-stationery-office.co.uk/pa/cm/cmhansrd.htm (372)

Previous day's session made available at 08:00. Online editions available since 1988–89 session.

Hansard (*House of Lords Daily Debates*)

http://www.parliament.the-stationery-office.co.uk/pa/ld/ldhansrd.htm (373)

Previous day's session made available at 08:00. Online editions available since 1995–96 session.

HM Inspectorate of Prisons

http://www.homeoffice.gov.uk/cpg/hmiprispage.htm (374)

Annual and other reports.

HM Inspectorate of Probation

http://www.homeoffice.gov.uk/cpg/hmiprobhome.htm (375)

Annual and other reports.

House of Commons Home Page

http://www.parliament.uk/commons/HSECOM.HTM (376)

A considerable volume of information relating to the current legislative activities of the House, its committees, proceedings, membership, and the non-parliamentary interests of members is made available. All the important publications relating to its deliberations are accessible online. These include a daily summary agenda and order of business, questions arranged by day, the complete text of all the public bills before the House, Hansard, the record of daily proceedings in the chamber, the full text of Standing Committee debates on bills, and reports of the Standing Committees.

There is also a substantial volume of information available relating to individual members, to political party groupings, on membership of the government and the opposition, on membership of Standing Committees, and information on by-elections. To get to this information you need to select the link to *Information about the House of Commons Members of Parliament*, and then *List of Members and Ministers*. The link to *Her Majesty's Government* provides information on members of the cabinet, ministers by department of state, and an alphabetical listing of members of the government. There is also information available on the opposition and other parties.

Also available from this site is the *Register of Members' Interests*, and links to all the Standing Committees. From their Home pages you can establish membership and access reports. The *Fact Sheets* provide information on various aspects of the proceedings of the House.

House of Lords Home Page

http://www.publications.parliament.uk/pa/ld/ldhome.htm (377)

The information available parallels in large measure that which is provided through the House of Commons Web presentation. The daily proceedings, Select Committee reports, standing orders, and public bills are all accessible. There is also a guide to the proceedings of the Lords.

The House of Lords judgments have been available online since 14 November 1996. These can be downloaded by selecting the link to Judicial work and judgments, *http://www.publications.parliament.uk/pa/ld/ldjudinf.htm* (378).

Other files from this page provide details on the judicial work of the House of Lords.

Immigration Appellate Authority

http://www.iaa.gov.uk/ (379)

Information on the appeals procedure and its workings.

Immigration and Nationality Directorate

http://www.ind.homeoffice.gov.uk/ (380)

A division of the Home Office, the site provides information on immigration and asylum issues, including work permits, applying for British nationality, breaking policy news, obtaining immigration advice, legislation applicable to asylum (1951 UN Convention on the Status of Refugees, Immigration and Asylum Act 1999), and the appeals procedure. Also available are online forms and links to agencies providing advice and support, and statistics relating to asylum.

Information Commissioner

http://www.dataprotection.gov.uk/ (381)

The Information Commissioner enforces and oversees the Data Protection Act 1998 and the Freedom of Information Act 2000.

Intellectual Property

http://www.intellectual-property.gov.uk/ (382)

UK government portal, targeted primarily at consumers.

Law Commission for England and Wales

http://www.lawcom.gov.uk (383)

Reports and consultation papers available.

Legal Services Commission

http://www.legalservices.gov.uk/ (384)

News, reports, forms, manuals, acts, budgets, and calculations relevant to the Community Legal Service and the Criminal Defence Service.

Lord Chancellor's Department

http://www.lcd.gov.uk/lcdhome.htm (385)

The Home page links to resources concerning varied facets of the legal system and the administration of justice in England and Wales, and includes many documents and reports. Some of the more important headings under which they are arranged are: civil matters, criminal law, data protection, the courts, judges and QCs, legal aid and conditional fees, magistrates, and human rights.

National Assembly for Wales

http://www.wales.gov.uk/ (386)

Northern Ireland Assembly

http://www.ni-assembly.gov.uk/ (387)

Northern Ireland Legislation

http://www.northernireland-legislation.hmso.gov.uk/ (388)

Access to the full text of legislation relating to Northern Ireland, including Acts of the Northern Ireland Assembly, statutory rules of Northern Ireland, Northern Ireland Orders in Council and links to acts of the UK Parliament and UK statutory instruments that apply specifically to it.

Official-Documents.co.uk

http://www.official-documents.co.uk/ (389)

Command Papers, House Papers, Departmental Papers and Reports. Divided into two sections by a tab at the top: 1994–2001 and 2002.

Official Solicitor and Public Trustee

http://www.offsol.demon.co.uk/ (390)

Patent Office: UK

http://www.patent.gov.uk/ (391)

See 9.16 Subject areas – Intellectual property.

Public Bills before Parliament

http://www.parliament.the-stationery-office.co.uk/pa/pabills.htm (392)

Complete text of public bills currently under consideration by parliament.

Scotland Legislation

http://www.scotland-legislation.hmso.gov.uk/ (393)

Coverage similar to that for the Northern Ireland legislature, documented above.

Scottish Law Commission

http://www.scotlawcom.gov.uk/ (394)

Scottish Legal Aid Board

http://www.slab.org.uk/ (395)

Scottish Legal Services Ombudsman

http://www.slso.org.uk/ (396)

Scottish Parliament

http://www.scottish.parliament.uk/ (397)

Statutory Instruments of the UK

http://www.legislation.hmso.gov.uk/stat.htm (398)

The texts that are available online date from 1987.

UK Members of Parliament 2001

http://www.psr.keele.ac.uk/area/uk/mps.htm (399)

Compiled by Richard Kimber, University of Keele. The listing by constituency provides information on the election results, candidates, votes cast for each, percentage of the vote. A comparative table is provided for the 1997 election. To locate information by MP, use the *Find* option on the *Edit* menu, or access the alphabetical listing of MPs *http://www.psr.keele.ac.uk/area/uk/mpsorted.htm* (400).

UK Online

http://www.ukonline.gov.uk/ (401)

This is the official UK government portal, which provides links to Web sites providing information on UK central and local government activities. The home page is used primarily for announcements. The most useful page is probably *Quick Find*, which links to an A to Z of central government, an A to Z of local government, political parties, and a short topic index. For the Home pages of departments of state, agencies, etc., use the A to Z of central government.

United Kingdom Parliament

http://www.parliament.uk/ (402)

Links to House of Commons, House of Lords, and further information about Parliament's operations.

Wales Legislation

http://www.wales-legislation.hmso.gov.uk/ (403)

Statutory instruments made by the National Assembly for Wales, and acts of the UK Parliament and statutory instruments that apply primarily or exclusively to Wales.

Part IV

SUNDRY MATTERS

As the possibilities of Web design become more complex, it is not easy to find publications that focus predominantly on the elementary principles of Web design and page compilation. Many current publications that deal with Web design and compilation are lengthy, and heavy on technical detail and manipulation. In a short chapter it is only possible to provide the most essential information. I will, however, provide a list of very good online resources that will take you further along this road.

10.1 Introduction

Is HTML easy? Well, is mathematics, or physics, or sociology, or psychology, or anything else? It depends: on whom we are talking about relative to what we are talking about. The first volumes that appeared on the earliest version of HTML were very slim, a couple of hundred pages. The 1997 edition of *HTML 4.0 Unleashed*, from Sams Publishing, clocked in at 1030 sizeable pages. Even if it were easy to plough through, which it is not, it would not be possible for most of those reading this chapter to find the time, interest, need, or patience to do so.

The appropriate question is not 'is HTML easy?' which for most people in its most advanced forms it is probably not, but 'is the HTML that it is necessary for me to master in order to construct the Web pages that I need, within my competence and time constraints?' Jakob Nielsen, the author of *Designing Web Usability*[1] and one of the foremost authorities on Web design, has noted that

> Ultimately, users visit your website for its content. Everything else is just the backdrop. . . . Usability studies indicate a fierce content focus on the part of users. When they get to a new page, they look immediately in the main content area of the page and scan it for headlines and for other indications of what the page is about. . . . Content is number one.

This is even more so for academic-oriented sites and pages than it is for many others. Content is largely textual, so that the bulk of what is required can be compiled in a word processor, saved as an HTML file, and then *imported* into a Web page. The rest is largely systematic organisation, and the adding of Web value, in the form of hyperlinks, text formatting, page layout, and overall presentation.

10.2 Tools

It is possible to compile perfectly adequate, even sophisticated Web pages by using an ordinary word processor or text editor. You can compile Web pages using Notepad, Word, WordPerfect, or any other text editor. Nonetheless, it is undoubtedly considerably easier to do so with the aid of a dedicated software application that is called an *HTML editor*, which, essentially, is a sophisticated word processor for Web pages, the HTML equivalent of Microsoft's Word.

The Netscape browser suite has a built-in HTML editor called *Composer*, the interface of which is illustrated in Figure 10.1. In more recent versions of Netscape you access this from the *Tasks* menu. Although there are differences between versions in relation to some of the features, and where they are located, the basic features are available in all versions. The *Composer* that comes with Netscape 6.0 is a perfectly reasonable HTML editor that will enable you to compile basic Web pages with relative ease. Netscape can be downloaded from *http://www.netscape.com.*

If you do not want to use *Composer* there are other HTML editors that are available and also free of cost. The best place to locate them is the software archive *Tucows*, at *http://www.tucows.com*. You need to navigate through some

Figure 10.1

pages to find the HTML editors' listing. Select your operating system platform from the opening page, which for most people will be Windows. From the tabs at the top of the page select *Internet*, then select *HTML Editors* from the section *HTML Tools*. The pages that download will provide information on a number of HTML editors. Those that are designated *Freeware* do not cost anything. They are all quite similar in terms of functionality. Select those that have the highest ratings (numbers of cows) and try them out. Most of the other editors are *Shareware*, and are relatively inexpensive. You can usually try them out for 30 days without having to pay anything up-front.

In what follows I will assume that you will be using an HTML editor at some stage of Web page compilation.

It is not necessary to compose the bulk of text content in the HTML editor. You can do so in any word processor. To convert files that you have composed in Word into a Web page, open them, then from the *File* menu select *Save As . . .* and save them as a *Web Page/html document*, by choosing this option from the *Save as type . . .* in the *Save As . . .* dialog box. Having done this, to import the file into your HTML editor select *Open File* in *Composer*. In other HTML editors you may need to do this by selecting the *Import/File* from either the *File* or the *Insert* menu.

10.3 HTML *or* Hypertext Markup Language

Web pages are written in HTML or, to be academically pedantic about it, their contents need to conform to HTML specifications to be viewed satisfactorily in

Web browsers. HTML is a markup not a programming language. In other words, the markup tags that constitute HTML indicate to a browser how it should present the text; for instance, emboldened, italicised, in the middle of the page, in larger font, in coloured font, indented, etc. It is, therefore, primarily a presentational coding.

As noted below, many HTML editors can be used in the same way as you would employ a word processor. You type in the text, and add value to it in terms of formatting, and tables and graphics, by using the toolbar buttons or the menu options. When conducting these operations you do not see on the screen the underlying HTML coding. Do you need, therefore, to know anything about such coding when compiling Web pages? After all, you cannot see the underlying coding for Microsoft Word but manage, for the most part, quite successfully, albeit occasionally with some frustration. In my experience it is difficult at times to compile and validate Web pages without a smattering of knowledge concerning certain aspects of HTML. Minimally, you need this in order to be able to determine why things are not working as you want them to; for instance, why when you select a hyperlink you receive a page with an error message rather than content. Although there are technicians, and help desks, that might be able to provide assistance, this takes time, and there are too few of these resources in most institutions relative to the rate of growth in demand for such assistance.

Raw HTML, or the source code, consists of instructions that are bounded by angle brackets < > which contain the tags. The < bracket opens the coding instruction, and > closes it. To see a page that includes HTML coding, open a Web page in your browser, preferably one without frames, and including text, and then select the *Edit* menu and choose the option *Page source/source*.

The bare bones of an HTML document, that is, the elements that must be included, are:

```
<html>
<title> </title>
<body>
[The text and images that are part of the main body of the page are placed here]
</body>
</html>
```

In other words, if you paste the above into a word processor and type text between the two *body* tags, and then save this as an HTML file, you will have a perfectly valid Web document that will display in a browser window as you intended.

Figure 10.3 displays the HTML coding of the text in Figure 10.2. I have inserted white space between the distinct components, for illustrative purposes.

A Short Biography of Jean Piaget

Jean Piaget (1896-1980)

Jean Piaget was born in Neuchâtel (Switzerland) on August 9, 1896. He died in
Geneva on September 16, 1980. He was the oldest child of Arthur Piaget, professor
of medieval literature at the University, and of Rebecca Jackson. At age 11, while he
was a pupil at Neuchâtel Latin high school, he wrote a short notice on an albino
sparrow. ...

Other Piagetian Web Resources

Jean Piaget Archives (Switzerland): www.unige.ch/piaget/

Jean Piaget Archives (Switzerland)

Figure 10.2

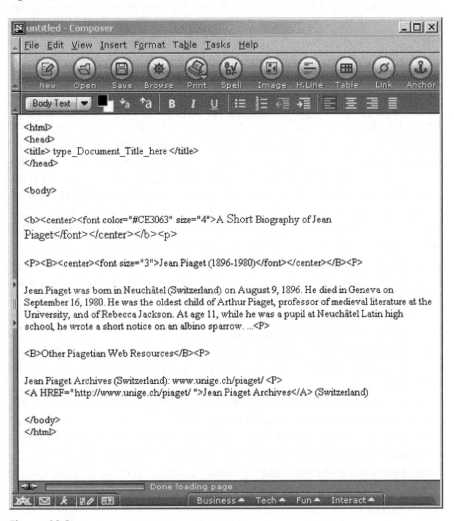

Figure 10.3

The spacing that appears in the text in Figure 10.3 will not appear in the HTML source coding, which is interspersed with line endings, but not white space.

The top part, known as the document header, comprises an opening <html> tag, signifying that this is an HTML document. The next component is contained between the opening and closing header tags, <head> and </head>. In between the opening and closing tags is inserted the document title, and, in more advanced pages than of the sort that I am dealing with here, coding and other document information.

Note that for many HTML instructions there are opening and closing tags, the latter signified by a forward slash before the tag text to which it applies, as in </head>. There are some tags that do not need to be closed, as, for instance, the paragraph tag <p>, which does not require the use of the closing tag </p>, the inclusion of which is optional. If the instructing tag does require closing, as do the italics tag <i> and the emboldening tag <b>, then all text succeeding that instruction will be italicised or emboldened respectively, until the closing tag is encountered. So, if you preview your Web page, and find that somewhere along the content, the rest of the text is italicised, emboldened, or hyperlinked, this will most probably be because you missed out the closing tag. Locate the point where the formatting should change, and insert the closing tag.

The only thing of interest in the header, in the context of the level of HTML that I am discussing here, is the document title, which should be inserted between the opening and closing <title> tags, indicated in Figure 10.3 by *type_Document_title_here*. The HTML title is not and need not be the same as the document title. For instance, the document title might be *The Assassination and Trial of Jean-Paul Marat as Performed by the Inmates of the Asylum of Charenton, etc* which you might shorten to *The Trial of Marat*, or *Marat/Sade play* for the HTML title. *It is important* to pay attention to the content of the HTML document title because it is this that is picked up by search engine robots and subsequently parsed for database use. It should be descriptive of the content but not unduly long, as this reduces the volume of content of the document displayed to users in search engine query returns.

The second main component of the HTML document is the body, contained between the opening <body> and closing </body> tags. This is where most of the content visible in the browser window is included. The HTML document closing tag is the closing HTML tag </html> which signifies that this is the end of the document.

Many HTML editors, including *Composer*, are referred to as being WYSIWYG, which stands for *What You See is What You Get*. You type your text, just as in an ordinary word processor, add value, say font colour, italics, and emboldening, in the same manner as you do in a word processor, such as Word, by blocking relative sections, and then selecting menu options or toolbar buttons. You do not need to manually insert the relevant HTML tags; this is done automatically.

In Figure 10.3, some of the components of the button bars will be familiar from a word processor, for instance, new, open, save, print, bold, italics, spell, alignment, and indentation. To learn how to use these features, and what others are available in your HTML editor, open a new page (button or file menu) and experiment. Type some text, or paste in some paragraphs from another document that you have already word processed. Block some of it, and start experimenting: italicise, embolden, colour the font (font menu), etc., doing this on different portions of the text. Open menus and see what is on them.

When you have added some features, *preview* the document, the feature usually being included on the *View* or *File* menu, which displays your text in the browser window. The preview feature shows you exactly how the document will look in a similar Web browser if uploaded on to a Web server and accessed from there. *Composer* previews the document in Netscape; most other HTML editors give you the option of previewing in either Netscape or Internet Explorer. *Always* preview in both of these, as there can be subtle differences in how they appear. Some HTML editors give you the additional option of previewing in different size screens, which it is also advisable to do. Many people may be using screens that are smaller than the one that you use when compiling your page. What on your screen may appear to be aesthetically satisfactory and uncluttered may appear on a smaller screen to be less satisfactory.

10.4 Page layout

In many Web presentations there is a difference between the Home page, and the rest, the former frequently including more elaborate graphics, occasionally a search engine, links to other pages, navigational aids, Web counters, and minimal text. It is too complex to cover this type of page here. I assume an introductory page with links to other pages that is minimalist in graphic design characteristics, and other pages that are not markedly discrepant in structure, layout, and presentation. These other pages in the presentation I presume to be largely composed of text with hyperlinks and some graphics if required.

For an elaborate Home page it is worth considering getting someone else to compile this for you, even if you have to pay for it. Most institutions of higher education have dedicated Web design personnel who can produce page templates, which you fill in with your own content. If not, consider looking at some books on Web design; there are enough ghastly Web pages out there already and you surely do not want to add to their numbers.[2] Some HTML editors, *FrontPage*, for instance, come with some templates, which few seem to use, probably for very good reasons.

The elements of page layout that you should be particularly attentive to are margins, background image and colour, inter- and intra-page navigation, page length, organisation, and authorship.

10.5   Tables

In HTML there is no facility for page margins, and, minimal coding for positioning text or graphics, although blocks of text can be centred, or aligned left or right. Most Web designers and page compilers have from the outset considered this to be a major impediment. They have overcome this limitation by using tables.

As you can divide up the page into an infinite number of rows and columns, in principle you can position text or graphics anywhere you like on a page by inserting them into an appropriate table cell. There is no limit on the number of tables that you can include in a Web page. So, if you want to position three graphics in a row at designated positions, followed by text, followed by some more graphics, then text, etc., you can accomplish all this by the use of tables. Similarly, if you wanted to give your page a newspaper column effect, you would do this by having two or more parallel one-row/one-column tables, as shown in Figure 10.4.

HTML table features are many: they allow you to colour particular cells, to have borders of varying widths and colours, or none at all, to have margins (cell padding), to align the text horizontally and vertically, among others. If

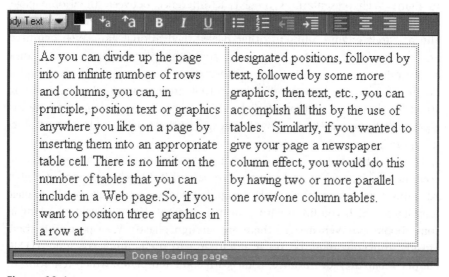

Figure 10.4

you want to insert a graphic into a cell, you place the cursor in it, and use the *Insert* menu to select *picture/graphic*, and then select one from those available on your storage media; alternatively, a graphic can be copied into memory and pasted in.

The manifold features of tables are too involved to elaborate on here. It is a lot more complicated to relay in print than it is to comprehend in practice. Fifteen minutes of experimentation, following ten minutes of reading the instructions relating to tables in the help files of the HTML editor, should be enough to provide a degree of familiarity with the more essential elements. Here are some pointers to bear in mind:

- Specify the height and width of tables in percentages rather than pixels, and do the same for cells, as absolute screen sizes vary.

- Generally, HTML table borders are ugly and unnecessary. To get rid of them, set border width to 0. Setting this to 0 does not eliminate the cell and table outlines when working with the HTML editor, so that you can easily observe the effects of your layout. When you preview the table the outline lines will no longer be visible.

- In order to set various cell features, such as text/graphic horizontal and vertical alignment, click with the right mouse button in the cell, which will bring up a dialog box that enables cell feature alteration.

- In order to set table features, place the cursor just touching the border of the table (not cell), and right click, which will bring up a dialog box that enables table feature alteration.

- In many HTML editors, once you have selected the number of rows and columns, you can alter the width of columns and rows by dragging their outline borders.

10.6 Margins

Text that covers the whole width of the browser window is more difficult to read, and aesthetically less pleasing, than text that has margins at either side. As HTML does not provide a margins feature, using tables can achieve this. If you want to display text with all-round margins, as in a printed page, create a table with one row and one column. For a page that will look like that of a printed page, generally specify that the table width should be 80–90 per cent, and the vertical height 80–85 per cent, as illustrated in Figure 10.5.

Having inserted your content, if it does not fit your requirements exactly with the initial table size specifications, alter these until they do meet them by right clicking in the table, and selecting *table properties/features*.

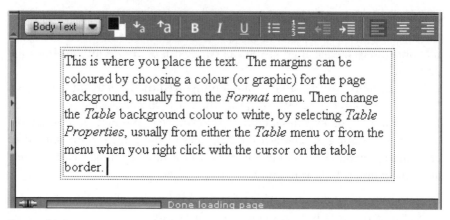

Figure 10.5

10.7 Page background

It is difficult to provide positive general guidance on page backgrounds owing to vast differences in aesthetic taste, and the objectives of the presentation. If your goal is to provide a few pages of announcements, or non-annotated links to resources relating to a particular topic/discipline, the background is less critical than when providing a resource heavy in textual content. If those accessing the pages in question are expected to read large chunks of text and absorb their contents, then it is very important to ensure that text is legible and that it is, from a cognitive psychological point of view, easy to read. White text, in particular fonts against a black background, can be very striking; it is, however, extremely difficult to read large amounts formatted in this way. The same applies to many other combinations of coloured fonts and backgrounds. It is reasonable to assume that black print on a white background is, for most purposes, the easiest combination of background and foreground for most people to read, otherwise most text would not be presented in this way.

There is no need, however, to confine the pages to black text against a white background, which is not very interesting, particularly when reading on-screen. You can set a left margin to a different colour by inserting a table with one row and three columns: the right and left columns each being about 7.5 per cent of screen width, and the middle one being where you place your text and graphics. To select a colour for the left column/margin, right click in it and select *Cell Properties*, or select this from the *Table* menu, and then select *Colour*, or *Table and Cell Background*, or equivalent. You can also place a graphic in the left column for the margin. To implement this, insert the cursor in the top left-hand corner, and from the *Insert* menu select *Insert Image/Picture*.

It is far easier to specify what it is inadvisable to do respecting page background than to advocate a particular combination of features that work reasonably well.

- Don't fill pages with animations and blinking segments of text; most users find both irritating, and they distract from the message that you want to convey.

- With very few exceptions, limited generally to Home/first pages of a presentation, background images, unless they are a very light pastel colour, distract from the content, and are soon found tiring and tiresome. Some images make it extremely difficult to read the accompanying text, conveying the impression that the text is there to accompany the image rather than the other way around. Various textured images fit into this category.

10.8 Page length

Here too, individual preferences come into play. There are, however, a few factors that you should take into consideration.

- Try to ensure that a page does not take more than 30 seconds to download over a 28.8 modem, unless the page is designed to be accessed on an organisation's Intranet. Some HTML editors, *FrontPage* for instance, provide information on download times of pages that are in the interface composition window.

  Figure 10.6 displays download times for different sizes of pages. The most common modem speeds currently in use are rated at a maximum of 28.8 and 57 Kbps, with most users experiencing download transmission speeds of between 26.6 and 44 Kbps. It is for such speeds that you should largely seek to cater.

- In my opinion a substantial body of text should not be presented over a large number of pages, each of which provides only a few moderate-sized

		Ideal download times (h:mm:SS)			
Connection	Transfer rate	50 KB	100 KB	500 KB	1 MB
14.4 Kbps modem	1.76 KB/s	0:00:28	0:00:57	0:04:44	0:09:43
28.8 Kbps modem	3.52 KB/s	0:00:14	0:00:28	0:02:22	0:04:51
33.6 Kbps modem	4.10 KB/s	0:00:12	0:00:24	0:02:02	0:04:10
56 Kbps modem	6.84 KB/s	0:00:07	0:00:15	0:01:13	0:02:30
128 Kbps ISDN	15.64 KB/s	0:00:03	0:00:06	0:00:32	0:01:06

Figure 10.6
Source: Netpanel.com

paragraphs. There are a substantial number of authors who present a text, which might be a report, an article, or even a book, distributed over innumerable pages, which means you have to be online for a substantial period of time, selecting the *next* page hyperlink in the series every 30 seconds. This is irritating for those who want to read online, and frustrating for those who want to save the text to disk to read offline, as numerous pages have to be saved. The added drawback is that the author has to construct and then test all these pages. At times the presentation may need to contain a substantial number of pages, but these should take about 30 seconds to download over a 28.8 Kbps modem.

■ Unless a graphic is important in the context of the presentation, or is very small in terms of *bytes*, consider excluding it. There are innumerable Home pages that take a long time to download, which include very fancy graphics, animations, Java applets, etc., these pages being mere entry points to those that users wish to view, and presenters wish to market. Many users simply don't bother dangling online. Although such pages might attest to the Webperson's technical and design proficiency, they serve very little other purpose, especially in scholarly presentations. If you want to maximise visitors to your site and enhance their satisfaction and probability of return visits, it is worth avoiding such extravagancies. There are online forums where Webpersons can ply the intricacies of their trade, where such proficiencies can be demonstrated and are much appreciated.

10.9 Page authorship/dating

For reasons that were discussed in Chapter 3, every page, even if part of a larger presentation, or a series (e.g. a text in parts), should have a reference to the author and should be dated. Some HTML editor packages include a dating feature that is automatically updated every time the page is modified. Preferably the author's email address, or that of the Webperson responsible, should be available on the page.

10.10 Navigation and hyperlinks

There are two types of hyperlinks: external and internal. An *external* hyperlink is a pointer to another Web page/HTML file. An *internal* hyperlink is a link to another place on the same page. An external hyperlink can point to a particular place on a specific page, rather than just the page. When the external hyperlink is not pointing to a particular part of the page, the top of the page will display in

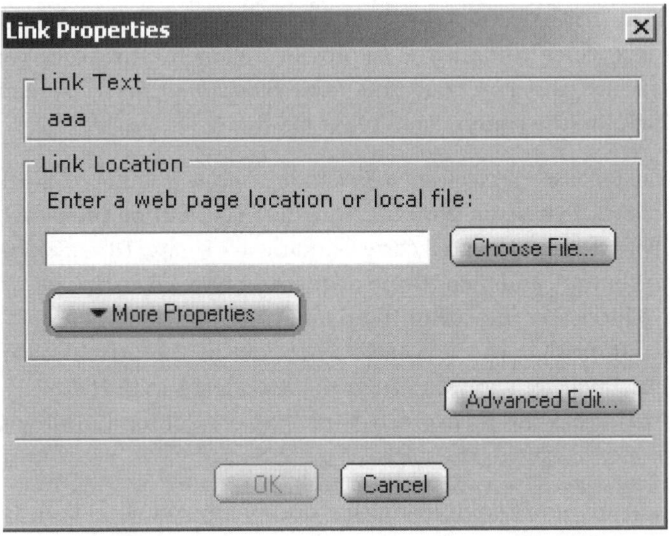

Figure 10.7

the browser window. When an external hyperlink points to a particular part of a page, the text/graphic to which it points will be displayed at the top of the browser window.

To create an external hyperlink, select the text by blocking it, or the graphic by clicking on it, and then select the (hyper)link button from the tool bar, the image of which frequently is a chain link. This will open a dialog box like Figure 10.7, or, as in *FrontPage*, similar to the familiar *Save As* . . . dialog box. Where the textbox refers to *Link Location* or, in other HTML editors, *URL*, insert the URL of the file that you want to link to. This file may be on your own server, or on an external one. An easy way of establishing this, if possible, is to download the file you want to link to in your browser, and then copy its URL from the Address box and paste it in. If you want to link to a new file, which you have not yet uploaded to the server, you can do the same, and then just alter the last component, the file name, manually.

To create a hyperlink from one part of your document to another, you have to create an *anchor* at the point that you want to link to. The order of operations is as follows:

1. Block the text/graphic at the point you want to link to. If using *Composer* select the *Anchor* button. For some unknown reason, developers of some other HTML editors refer to the *Anchor* tag as *Target* or *Bookmark*. You should be able to locate the appropriate command on the *Insert* menu on most editors.

2. When you have selected the *Anchor* button, you will be presented with a dialog box which will ask you to provide a name for the place you want to point to (i.e. the text that you have blocked). Choose a name that is meaningful in the context, and select OK.

3. Go to the place *where you want to link* to the *Anchor* point *from*. Block the text/ graphic, select the *Link* button/command. You will be presented, in *Composer*, with the dialog box corresponding to Figure 10.7. Select the *More Properties* button, and then the name that you have given the *Anchor*. In other HTML editors, the procedure is in principle the same, but the particular button/option that you will have to choose in the presenting dialog box varies. In *FrontPage* you select from the *Bookmark* list; in *HotDog* (yes, that is the name), from the *Named Target* list. Just click around until you find the name that you gave to the *Anchor*.

4. To link to an *Anchor* point in another document, you select both the file and the *Anchor/Target/Bookmark* associated with it.

5. The HTML tag coding for a link is <a href="URL">text/graphic</a> as in <a href="http://www.website.org/glossary.htm">glossary</a>. Every element of this is essential. Watch out particularly for missing opening and closing double inverted commas, and absence of the closing </a> tag. All this will be done automatically by the HTML editor, but sometimes you will need to check, due to typing errors, unnoticed deletions, etc.

6. The HTML tag coding for an *Anchor* is <a href="name [that you give the anchor]">prejudice</a>, as in <a href="prejudice">Prejudice</a>. The link to the anchor, *if in the same document*, will be <a href= "#prejudice"> Prejudice</a>. Although this will be done automatically, it should be checked. When you see a URL such as *http://www.website.org/ glossary.htm#prejudice*, the *#prejudice* indicates that the link is to a particular *Anchor* in the document, named *prejudice*.

One of the main advantages of hypertext is that the author is no longer dependent on sequential presentation; you can go off in innumerable directions through hyperlinks. This is an enormous advantage in enabling linking to resources supplementary to the main theme, but it is a feature that also requires some thought as to the resources linked to and the volume of hyperlinks. A page strewn with hyperlinks is likely to lose the reader's attention and make it difficult to conclude what the purpose of the author is, or what message the page is intended to convey. Hyperlinks should, therefore, be used sparingly; the author should only expect to draw on a small quantum of reader patience. Also, if you are perennially linking to resources that are far superior to those that you are providing, the reader has little incentive to delve deeper into your own contributions.

Finally, in addition to experimenting with using the HTML editor, one of the easiest and most rewarding ways to increase familiarity with HTML techniques and possibilities is learning from the millions of examples already available on the Web. If you see something that you want to emulate, or to understand how it is done, look at the source code of the documents concerned, by selecting *Source* from the *View* menu on the browser.

10.11 Marketing your pages

Generally, the object of compiling and publishing Web pages is to have them accessed and read. For reasons that have been discussed in other chapters, the probability of any particular Web page, especially those that are part of a new presentation, being accessed by chance is infinitesimally slight. There are billions of pages that can be accessed, pages that are recently published will not be hyperlinked to through other pages, and, consequently, unlikely to be trawled by search engine robot programs. The fewer the pages in the presentation, the less likely is it that any of them will be indexed by search engines.

There are a number of things that you can do to increase the visibility of your pages.

■ You can manually register your pages with the major search engines. Given that your pages are not hyperlinked to from others, the only way that your pages can be entered in the database of a search engine is if you enter the details yourself, or you take measures to ensure that they are.

There are companies, as well as software, that will undertake this task of publicising your pages to search engines. Details of pages will be *registered* with tens, if not hundreds, of search engines that are available. While I have not used such facilities myself, generally they constitute, in my opinion, an unnecessary expense. Utilising them will, in all probability, take up more of your time than is necessary to resort to the alternative, which is to manually register your pages with the top four or five search engines. Most referrals to pages come from search engines (between 85 and 90 per cent), and mainly from the four or five most popular engines. If you register your Home page with these, you will not achieve substantially less than if you were to have them marketed by someone else, or use software to achieve the same end. To register your Home or other pages, access the search engine, and locate a link to *submit your URL/submit your site*. You may have to search around a bit as this usually is not the most visible feature on its Home page, if not buried deeper down. Despite my earlier lukewarm comments about Yahoo, many access it regularly, so it would probably be worth registering pages here as well. At the bottom of the Yahoo Home page, *http://www.yahoo.com*, select the link to *How to Suggest a Site*.

■ Another approach is to target your publicity to specific audiences. First, you need to clarify who are the target audiences. Next, establish the Net presence forums through which they can be reached. Mailing lists and newsgroups are obvious starting points. Sending a message to either announcing a resource that might be of interest is a good way of reaching specialised audiences. A more direct approach is to obtain the email addresses of the target audience and email them. Many professional associations make available online the email addresses of members. More time-consuming, but not entirely impractical in the UK, is to obtain relevant email addresses by accessing university faculties/departments/schools, and locating the email addresses of potentially interested staff.

■ A third method is to directly contact the editors/Web personnel of subject gateways that your presentation is likely to fall under, informing them of its content and URL. It usually helps if you have included a reference to their site in your presentation. The degree to which this latter is necessary depends on how significant your Web presentation is in the context of the online corpus. If it is original material that is perceived as being significant, not being replicated elsewhere, it is likely that the subject gateway editor will create a link to it irrespective of reciprocity. Nonetheless, it is worth remembering that reciprocity is the thread that links much of the Web, and substantial goodwill can be gained by it. Having your pages referenced from subject gateways will increase their visibility to search engine robots, as well as to users accessing them. The same logic applies to other sites/pages that deal with similar or related subject matter to that which your pages reference.

The more pages that your own are linked to, the higher your Net visibility, and the more accesses to them that are likely to result. You should attempt to monitor the volume of activity on your pages, which you can do in a number of ways:

■ Monitor the Web logs. In order to do this you will need to contact your system administrator unless you control the Web server. It may not always be possible to easily monitor activity from the logs unless your Web pages are configured on the server in a particular way. Discussion of this issue is beyond the scope of this book.

■ Install a hit counter on your pages. Personally I don't like these very much, but if there is no alternative, select one that does not look too conspicuous. There are many that are available without charge: enter *hit counter* or *Web counter* in Google. Instructions on how to install and incorporate these into your Web pages are usually provided. Some, such as one of Microsoft's free products, email you stats at intervals that you choose.

- You can monitor the number of other pages that are linked to yours through Google. Enter the URL of one of your pages in the Google query box and hit Enter. In the page that is returned select *Find web pages that link to* (your URL). When you select this link the pages are listed, their number being enumerated in the graphic bar near the top of the page. Obviously, this only lists those pages that are in the Google database. Nonetheless, this is a very useful feature as it enables you to establish: (1) how many pages are linked to yours, and (2) their perceived importance in terms of subject/topic specification. Some of these pages may include annotations that provide valuable feedback.

10.12 Basic considerations of Web page/Web site design

Prior to actually writing content there are a number of things that are worth considering with a view to reducing expenditure of time over the medium to long term. These considerations mostly concern those whose interest is in medium- to long-term presence, that is, those who want the presentation to remain on the Web and, generally, be added to periodically:

- Be very clear as to what the objectives of providing the information on the Web are, as these should dictate presentation, organisation of the materials, and the content. Think ahead to what you want to present in the long term, rather than just what you can manage to do at present, as subsequent reorganisation is likely to prove costly in time.

- Decide which server you want to store your Web pages on. For those who are undertaking a Web-based project while students, the university or college server is the obvious answer, and, in any event, will probably be a requirement. The project is not likely to be very substantial in terms of the number of pages, or intricate in terms of its sub-divisions, so even if you want to maintain/expand the presentation on the Web subsequent to the completion of your studies, moving this to another server is unlikely to be onerous or complex.

    For academic staff the decision is more complex. The university server has various advantages over those of Internet Service Providers (ISPs). It is free, uploading files from the network is usually quite straightforward, which might not be the case with ISPs, the university IT staff will be more likely to cater for specialist requirements than an ISP, and the Web pages can usually be integrated easily with other applications, such as conferencing systems and course management software. If the objective is to provide online materials for your own students taking particular courses, and not for wider dissemination, this should be the preferred option.

On the other hand, if you are building up a Web presentation in a particular field, probably related to your area of specialisation, and you anticipate having a lengthy academic career ahead of you, serious consideration should be given to registering your own domain name (e.g. *identity.com/ warlaws.info*), and storing your materials on an ISP server.

My reasons for this are related not to the difficulties of moving materials, but to marketing and intellectual property rights considerations. The objective of a Web presentation is for people to access the materials/site. Obtaining a significant Web presence in a particular field has two components. First, that it is linked to and positively evaluated by other Web presentations that are accessed by large numbers of people, particularly to major sites in the particular field it is focused on. Second, that the site/pages are high up on lists of hits returned from queries submitted to the most frequently used search engines that relate to the field it is focused on.

To illustrate: one of my sites, the Web Genocide Documentation Centre, as the name suggests, focuses on comparative genocide. Entering genocide in the search engine Google returned it as second in a list of 473,000 entries, and as 20th in AltaVista's (worldwide) list of 302,986 hits (14 December 2001). Being number 472,999 in Google, or 302,985 in AltaVista, would be extremely undesirable, as no one would bother to get there. You should aspire to be within the first 50, at worst. To move this site would be a major undertaking, as hundreds, if not thousands, of other Web sites would have to be informed so that they could modify their links, and it would take some time before the search engines had registered the new URLs as favourably as the old ones. My site has only been online for 5 years; had it been for 10 or, in the future, 20 years, the problem would be much greater.

Then there is the issue of intellectual property rights. If you place materials on a university Web server, you should first enquire as to who owns the materials that you have uploaded and compiled. Some institutions are persuaded that teaching materials belong to them, and there are some doubts concerning other categories of data uploaded. Placing materials on the server of an ISP avoids some of these issues.

- Ensure that links from one page to another in your presentation are formulated as *relative* URLs rather than *absolute* URLs. An absolute URL is one that includes the domain name of the server, for instance, http:// www.myinstitution.ac.uk/myfile.htm. For instance, if you link from one of your files, say *myfile1.htm* to another, *myfile2.htm*, and both are in the same directory, you should formulate the link as *myfile2.htm*, and not as http:// www.myinstitution.ac.uk/myfile2.htm. As the files are in the same directory, the server will automatically add http://www.myinstitution.ac.uk/ when someone clicks on the link. This way, when you move your files you will not need to rewrite all the links.

- If you envisage having, in the long run, a large presentation, with many files, you should carefully devise a directory structure so that not all the files are in the same directory, just as you have different directories for different types of file, or different purposes, on your hard drive. This has a twofold purpose: first, it allows you to find particular files easily; second, it makes it much easier to establish which parts of the presentation are being accessed most heavily, or which are returning errors, by examining Web logs.

10.13 Online sources of information on Web page compilation and design

Web Developers Journal
http://www.webdevelopersjournal.com/

Web Developer's Virtual Library
http://wdvl.internet.com/WDVL/About.html

Web Page Construction Tutor
http://www.bhs-ms.org/webhelp/writing.html

Web Page Construction Using Composer
http://www.csulb.edu/~jvancamp/composer.html

Notes

1. Nielsen, J., *New Riders*, Indianapolis, Indiana, 2000, pp. 99–100.
2. See Siegel, D., *Creating Killer Web Sites*, Hayden, 1997. Considered to be one of the best Web design books, but perhaps somewhat advanced. See also, Flanders, V. and Willis, M., *Web Pages that Suck*, Sybex International, 1998; although some of the information it provides is useful, the organisation of the book suffers from some of the flaws it identifies in Web pages. Nonetheless, while I would not recommend purchasing it, a library loan is justified. Siegel's book is rated very highly among Web designers, and if this is likely to be a continuing interest, it is more than worthy of purchase.

11

Miscellaneous computing matters

11.1 Keyboard shortcuts

It is a source of wonderment that many PC users, some who have been working on PCs for extended periods, are still unfamiliar with keyboard shortcuts for operations that they carry out often. Many users continue to implement procedures employing menus or toolbar buttons, when they could be executed much more rapidly and easily by using the keyboard.

- *Block Page*: Ctrl and a. With the cursor anywhere on the page press both keys simultaneously. Once blocked, you can use the copy and paste shortcuts (see below) to transfer the information to another application, or to another document within an application.

- *Bold*: Ctrl and b. Block the text, and press both keys.

- *Bookmark Page*: Ctrl and d. In both Communicator and IE, pressing both simultaneously will bookmark the page.

- *Copy*: Ctrl and c. Block text and then press both keys simultaneously. Use this to copy URLs by placing the cursor in the Location/Address box and then selecting both keys.

- *Cut (Delete)*: Ctrl and x. Block the text and then press the two keys simultaneously. While deleting the blocked text, it stores it in memory until the clipboard is subsequently overwritten by a further *cut* or *copy* command. Thus, if you want to move a body of text somewhere else in the document, you can block it, use the Ctrl x facility to delete it, place the cursor where you want to paste it, and then use the Ctrl v feature to paste the text to the new position.

- *Italics*: Ctrl and i. Block text and then press both keys simultaneously.

- *Open History Pages*: Ctrl and h. In both Communicator and IE, pressing both simultaneously will open/close the history feature.

- *Open New Web Page*: Ctrl and n. In both Communicator and IE, pressing both simultaneously will open a new browser window with the same Web page loaded in it as the one that was already open.

- *Paste*: Ctrl and v. Place the cursor where you wish the material previously copied to clipboard to be pasted, and simultaneously depress both keys.

- *Save*: Ctrl and s. When you are working on a document, in all Microsoft applications, if you press down Ctrl and then s, the document is saved, if saved before, or the *Save As . . .* dialog box comes up for file name entry completion. This is much quicker than selecting the button, or the option from the *File* menu, and so much easier, that it is bordering on the foolish not to save your documents every five minutes, given past experience with the freezing of applications and the downing of networks.

11.2 Viruses

Essentially, viruses are software programs, or programming fragments, that are developed by computer literati who endeavour to demonstrate compiling skills to themselves, or their likeminded peers, by surreptitiously infiltrating these onto PCs or servers. Some of these are benign. Others are not, costing the PC user community billions of pounds, while earning anti-virus software companies billions in turn. These can shut down PCs and servers, impede Internet connectivity, wipe disks, and distribute files on a computer across the Internet to other users. Microsoft products are particularly susceptible to such depredations.

The watchwords here are: protect, update, be extremely wary of strangers bearing attachments, and keep informed. Tedious, expensive, and irritating though it is, it is highly desirable that an anti-virus program should protect your PC. Universities and most medium-sized to large companies deploy these on their networks as a matter of course, and it is frequently not necessary, therefore, to do anything because this is automatically taken care of by the way in which the program has been configured on the network. If your personal computer does not have an anti-virus program installed, you should acquire one. There are a number of anti-virus programs available. You can consult one of the sources referenced below where their respective merits and costs are analysed. In weighing up whether or not you should acquire such a program, if one is not resident on your PC, you should consider the potential damage if you do not. The worst-case scenario is the destruction of all the files on your computer, and on some of your mobile storage media (floppy, external drives, zip disks, and writable CDs), requiring a reinstallation of the operating system and software programs, and the loss of all other files on the PC, as well as on other storage media that may have been contaminated through use on it.

The protection afforded by anti-virus programs has to be regularly updated. New viruses appear frequently. By the time you purchase a PC with an installed anti-virus program, other viruses will have appeared that it cannot recognise and *disinfect*. You need to access the Web site of the company that produced the program in order to download the latest updates to combat new viruses, known as anti-virus signature files. Usually you will find information on installation of these updates once you have downloaded them, and/or from the site where you accessed these. Such updating needs to be carried out at regular intervals, *at least once a month*. ZD Net has a page from which downloads of a range of manufacturers' latest files can be accessed, at ***http://www.zdnet.com/downloads/topics/antivirus.html***.

The most common way of spreading viruses today is through attachments to email messages. In principle, you should not open these directly. You should save them to disk and then run the anti-virus software on the disk prior to opening the attachments. In the case of entirely new viruses, or viruses which are not dealt with by your software because you have not updated it, the program will not be able to disinfect the files. It is, therefore, good practice not to open any attachments from sources with which you are not familiar. If you receive messages with an attachment, but without any clarification in the message body as to what they are, it is better to be cautious and reply to the sender requesting information as to their contents. It is possible for messages to be sent within some networks without any header information, that is, information concerning the sender, so you cannot actually reply to the message. Any messages that are received without a message body, and/or header information relating to who sent it, should be deleted. If it was a genuine message, the sender will in all probability get back to you subsequently.

The most dangerous type of attachment to open is what is known as an *executable* file, a file that opens up a program/application. These have the suffixes *exe, com, vbs*. It is not advisable to open files with these extensions unless you are *100 per cent certain* whom they came from, preferably that you had requested that these be sent to you. Opening unsolicited executable attachments is asking for trouble. Similar caution should be exercised in relation to the downloading of software programs, necessarily executables, from newsgroups and other bulletin boards. It is preferable to download these from the companies that produce them, or from reputable distributors on the Internet, such as Tucows, *http://www.tucows.com*.

For more information see the following online anti-virus resources:

- *Special Edition: Computer Viruses* (Northern Light) *http:// special.northernlight.com/compvirus/* Provides a wealth of information on the subject, including anti-virus solutions, current information, and diagnostics, which allows you to download software to test your vulnerability, etc. At the bottom of the page there is an Anti-Virus Solutions section that provides links to the main anti-virus software companies.

- *Virus Encyclopedia http://www.cai.com/virusinfo/encyclopedia/* 'This is the Virus Zoo. It contains information on viruses that are considered to be *in the wild.*' By *in the wild* is meant viruses that have infected PCs, and are 'out there'. Arranged alphabetically, this resource provides information on thousands of viruses. The information details the problems that a particular virus causes, the source of the infection, and how it is packaged (e.g. the message that accompanies it, if applicable).

  This is an extremely useful site. In addition to information on viruses, including a special section on *recent* ones, it also provides information on *hoaxes*, which are messages that are spread, typically by email, which claim that some threat exists to PCs from viruses, or similar, which do not in fact exist, and *Trojans*, which are malicious programs that masquerade as legitimate ones to infiltrate and then damage your system.

11.3 Frames, bookmarking, and URLs

Frames are an HTML feature that allows the screen to be divided into a number of windows, each of which has a separate file/document uploaded in it. You frequently encounter these where one of the frames is an index to contents. When you select one of the links in it, a corresponding document is uploaded in the adjacent window.

One of the major difficulties faced by users in connection with *framed* Web presentations is that of identifying their URLs and bookmarking them. When you are viewing files in a framed presentation, if you select a link, the associated file usually opens in the *parent* frame. This means that the URL that is displayed in the Location/Address box is not altered from that which was displayed prior to the selection. Consequently, if you want to bookmark the document that you have opened in the frame, you cannot just click on *Favorites/Bookmarks* and then select the *Add . . .* option, as it is the parent frame that would be bookmarked.

There are a number of ways of getting around these problems:

- You can open the document that is in the frame in a new window. This is particularly desirable if you want to follow up links from it. If you don't open it up in a new window, documents selected will still open in the parent frame. Place the mouse cursor over the document and right click. From the menu choose *Open Frame in New Window*. This usually works in both IE and Netscape. However, I have found that at times it does not work in IE, in which case follow the second procedure. Right click on the document and select *Properties*. This opens up a *Properties* information box. One of the entries is the URL (Address). Block this address with the mouse cursor, copy it by selecting Ctrl and c, click in the Address box of the browser window, and paste it in by selecting Ctrl and v. When you hit the Enter key, the document will begin to download in a new window.

- If you want a document that appears in a frame to appear in a browser window of its own, rather than in the parent frame, place the cursor over the link, right click, and select *Copy Shortcut* (in IE). Next, place the cursor in the Address box and press Ctrl and v, which will paste the URL into it. Hit Return. This will open the document in a new window.

- If all you want to do is bookmark the file that is linked to, when you right click over the link you can also select *Add to Favorites*. In Netscape, you can, similarly, right click on the link and select either *Add Bookmark* or *Open in New Window*. You can also bookmark the file from within the parent frame, in both IE and Netscape, by right clicking on the document and selecting *Add Favorites/Add Bookmarks* respectively. Note: you *must* click in the actual document, not in the surrounding parent frame/s.

11.4 Clearing your tracks: your PC and personal privacy

Article 8 of the European Convention on Human Rights is directed at drawing the parameters of private and family life. The Commission on Human Rights has referred to *private life* as the 'right to live, as far as one wishes, protected from publicity'. This right, as Merrills and Robertson note,[1] is clearly infringed 'if the authorities keep an individual under surveillance, maintain a record of his activities, investigate his financial affairs, tap his telephone, or check his mail'. Many who have PCs at home use them for a wide range of activities, including communication with others, financial management, business, recreation, purchasing, etc. The various activities that Merrills and Robertson refer to above occur increasingly via keyboard entries that are mediated by the storage mechanisms of a PC.

Governments, particularly in the UK and the USA, and the EU Commission, have for some years been endeavouring to introduce legislation that would enable them to monitor electronic mail and obtain access to files, under specified circumstances, that are located on digital storage media. The USA for years imposed restrictions on the exporting of encryption software with particular features, on the grounds that not to do so would hamper its abilities to combat crime, terrorism, and subversion. After the 11 September attack on the World Trade Center, governmental concerns relating to these matters have been heightened. Some recent reports indicate that in the UK government agencies are seeking the cooperation of Internet Service Providers in scrutinising their Web, mail, and FTP server logs.

Personal computers, as well as networked PCs, provide administrators and storage recovery experts with extensive means of establishing what precisely the user has been downloading, viewing, and accessing on private networks and the Internet. Few users of PCs are aware of the multiple tracks left by their keyboard entries, file manipulations, downloads, mailings, dialup activities, etc., on their computer. Occasionally this comes to light, as it did when the former UK pop star Gary Glitter's PC was scrutinised by technicians working for Personal Computer World, to whom he had brought it for attention.

The sections below provide information on how to delete *the more obvious traces*. Most logging of activities is stored on the hard disk that the operating system is installed on, invariably the drive designated C. It is not possible to provide details below that will cover every application and eventuality. You need to poke around a bit and record consciously what ordinarily you would probably take for granted. So, to cover your tracks, you should open the folders on the C drive, and look at files with names such as *cleanup*, *recent*, and *history*. You can open these, delete the contents, and save them before closing them again. Don't forget that many applications are configured to include a list of the last four to nine files that you accessed with them; these file names will remain listed even if the files themselves have been deleted, if these were the most recent ones uploaded.

(1) File deletion

Computer work, in terms of its tracking functions, is the equivalent of permanently creating a wax or vinyl phonograph record. Everything you do is recorded and logged somewhere. Many users are under the impression that deleting a file erases its contents irretrievably. It does not. Moreover, even if you could erase the file irretrievably with the Delete function, a record of that file's presence will be found elsewhere. Experts with appropriate hardware and software can sometimes, for instance, retrieve content from PC storage media that have been severely fire damaged.

Deleting a file in Microsoft operating systems is a two-stage process. In the file management program Windows Explorer you highlight the file on the disk on which it is stored, right click, and select Delete from the menu. This moves the file to the *Recycle Bin*. If you click on the *Recycle Bin*, the frame on the right will list the files in it. If you want to restore the file, you can right click on it and select *Restore*, which will make it available from the same location from which it was deleted. To delete the files permanently you need to select *Empty Recycle Bin* from the File Menu, or select the button in Windows 2000.

Once you have done that *you will not* be able to retrieve the files in question. However, **this does not mean that the files are no longer on your computer**. It is possible, with the relevant hardware and software, to retrieve these files. When a file is deleted, the segment on the disk that it occupied becomes vacant, but the file will not be irretrievable until such time as it has been entirely overwritten by other files occupying *all* the segments that it occupied. Consequently, you should be aware that if you pass your computer on to someone else, deleting your files is no guarantee that another person will not be able to retrieve them.

There are special software programs that can ensure that the files are permanently and irretrievably deleted. One of these is *CyberScrub*, ***http:// 165.121.190.90/home.html***. At this site you will find a table comparing its features with those of similar applications, enabling you to access these as well.

(2) Internet tracks

In order to access a file from a Web server you need, first, to insert an address in the *Address/Location* bar of the browser, or select a *Bookmark/Favorite*. From the moment you do this you begin to create a record of the sites that you have visited and the material that you have downloaded. Both IE and Netscape, by default, retain the URL of the addresses that you have recently visited in their *Address/Location* boxes. The page that you have downloaded will, by default, be retained in the browser's cache, and can be reloaded, and therefore viewed, by anyone with the requisite knowledge. The server that you have downloaded from may also have sent a *cookie* (see below), which is another marker of your visit. If you add a URL/page to *Bookmarks* or *Favorites*, another record of your viewing preferences and history is retained. IE and Netscape both maintain a record of your visits over a configurable period of time in the form of their *History* feature.

Singly and combined, all the above create footprints of your viewing habits and preferences. For various reasons, you may not want others to have access to this information. In the sections below I discuss issues associated with maintaining the privacy of user Internet surfing practices. Much of this applies in principle to other application usages. If you are working on networked PCs, particularly thin client machines that use applications from a central server, you may not be able to control many of the procedures detailed below.

It is not suggested here that you should continuously delete evidence of your Internet activity, or even do so at all. You should, however, be aware of the tracks you make and the information that is being collected about this, in case you wish to control access to these matters.

(2a) Deleting browsing history

The *History* facility tracks the identity (titles and URLs) of the pages that have been downloaded in a preconfigured period of time. To delete browser *History*, follow the steps below:

- *Netscape*: Select *Preferences* from the *Edit* menu and the *Clear History* button. You can also configure the number of days that your viewing history will be retained.

- *IE*: From the *Tools* menu select *Internet Options*, and then *Clear History* from the *General* tab. You can also configure the number of days that the history will be kept.

(2b) Deleting cache

By default both IE and Netscape allocate a specified volume of hard disk space to caching Web files that you have recently accessed. When the limit is reached, the oldest files are deleted to make room for those currently being downloaded. The purpose of the cache is to increase the efficiency of downloading pages. As many Web pages do not change from day to day, the browser retains copies of downloaded files on your hard disk. When you try to access a page that is in the cache the browser will upload the file from the cache rather than download it afresh, or check the file in the cache against that on the server. If there have been no changes, it will upload the file from the cache in preference, to speed things up. You can influence how the browser and cache interact by altering the cache configuration, as described below.

While speeding up Web activity, cached files are also a record of your viewing, and also take up disk space, which you may want to release. In IE, cached files are called *Temporary Internet Files*. You can delete these by selecting *Internet Options* from the *Tools* menu, and selecting *Delete Files* from the *General* tab. You can configure cache operation by selecting the *Settings* button, and then the volume of disk space allocated to caching, if any.

Since most PCs today have very sizeable disk storage capacities compared with that which they had five or six years ago, you can generally afford to be generous with the volume of space allocated to disk cache. In any event, with all browsers you can clear the cache easily if you run short of disk space, and reconfigure the space allocation at the same time.

In Netscape, the cache is accessed by selecting *Preferences* from the *Edit* menu. In the column on the left, click on the + to the left of *Advanced*, and then select *Cache*. There are two types of cache. *Memory Cache* refers to files that are in upper memory. This is automatically deleted every time you close the browser. It includes files that you have accessed since opening the browser, to the storage volume specified. If you download a lot of sizeable files it will soon start to be replenished with those most recently accessed. Generally, there is no need to clear the *Memory Cache*, unless an MI5 or MI6 agent rushes into the room in the midst of your browsing session. *Disk Cache* refers to files that are stored on your disk up to the volume of space specified. Selecting the appropriate buttons clears both Disk and Memory cache. You can also configure the size of the Disk cache.

(3) Cookies

The term *cookie* is employed to refer to information that is transmitted by the server from which you have downloaded a file/page to your computer. This is stored on your computer and activated when you subsequently access the same page – or sometimes other pages on the same site – to transmit/retransmit information about yourself or your preferences to the server. For instance, some online newspapers allow you to customise your preferences. You might be interested primarily in financial or sports information, but not information on politics and the arts. When you have configured your preferred profile for this site, a cookie will be sent to your browser that contains information relating to your preferences. When you close your browser down, the cookie will be stored on your hard disk. Next time you visit the site, the cookie containing the information on your preferences will be sent to the server, which will result in your profile preferences being executed so that you will initially see only the information in which you expressed an interest. Similarly, if you open an account with a commercial company, such as Amazon, information relating to you is stored in a cookie so that on your next visit relevant information will be accessible, such as your selections for possible future purchases. Even if you do not select any preferences, or open an account, servers will frequently send cookies.

Cookies, like Favorites, Bookmarks, History and cache files, and URLs in the Address and Location bars, are evidence of the sites that you have visited. Unfortunately, because there are differences relating to operating systems, browsers, and versions thereof, it is not possible to give details here of how you can delete these. Generally, however, if you open the file manager, *Explorer* for Microsoft operating systems, highlight the C drive, and select *Tools/Find/Files or*

Folders, or *Search*, depending on version, and enter the word *cookies* in the text box, this will retrieve a listing of the folders in which they are stored. Click on the folders to open them and delete; or click on the file and delete. You can obtain extensive information on various matters relating to cookies, including software that will allow you to manage them, from *cookiecentral.com* at *http://www.cookiecentral.com/*.

(4) Bookmarks/favorites

These files also track where you have visited on the Net. To delete particular Bookmarks:

■ *Netscape*: Select *Bookmarks/Manage Bookmarks*. Locate the particular bookmark, or folder, that you want to delete, right click on it, and select Delete from the menu options. If you want to delete all, click anywhere, press simultaneously Ctrl and a, which will block all the bookmarks, and select Delete from the *Edit* menu.

■ *IE*: Select *Favorites/Organize Favorites*. Locate the particular bookmark, or folder, that you want to delete, highlight it, and then select the Delete button. If you want to delete all Favorites, locate this folder on the C drive, using the procedures outlined in the above section on cookies.

(5) Location/address bar

When you insert an address in the *Location* or *Address* bar of Netscape or IE, respectively, the URL of a page is retained in them when you subsequently download another page. The purpose of this is to facilitate downloading the same page at some later point. Each browser has a default number of URLs that are *stored*. As you download subsequent pages, those earliest in the list are removed. Both browsers by this means keep a visible record of your recent viewing history.

To delete the *Location* bar addresses in Netscape, select *Preferences* from the *Edit* menu, and then *History/Clear Location Bar*. To remove the URLs from the IE *Address* bar, you need to clear the IE *History*. Select *Internet Options* from the *Tools* menu and, on the *General* tab, select *Clear History*, responding affirmatively to the message that appears.

(6) AutoComplete

The ever-helpful Microsoft Corporation has included in its browser software an AutoComplete facility. This is directed at saving the user time, and the need to look up URLs, form information, and passwords. If you have used a URL before, say *http://www.ess.uwe.ac.uk/genocide.htm*, when, on a subsequent occasion, you enter *www.e* the drop-down menu will highlight the remainder of the URL, or insert it in the *Address* text box, or apply the same to other URLs that you have downloaded before that begin with an *e* after the *www*. The AutoComplete facility also extends to forms and sites where you need to enter user-ids and passwords.

For the most part this is a very useful facility. However, it allows others to access the same sites, and to see the form information that you have provided, including personal details, if you start to type in the same details, say surname, first name, or address, of the person who initially used the PC.

To delete the AutoComplete information, select *Internet Options* from the *Tools* menu and then *AutoComplete* from the *Content* tab. Select the *Clear Forms* and *Clear Passwords* buttons, as required.

11.5 Downloading, installing, and uninstalling software

There are thousands of useful software applications that do not cost anything that can be downloaded. Downloading and installing software is usually easy and trouble-free. Having located a link to the file, double click on it. This will open the *Save* dialog box. You need to select a drive and directory/folder on your computer to which it will be downloaded. If downloading it at home, save it to the *temp* directory on your C drive, which is the drive on which the operating system is ordinarily installed. You can also download it to a floppy disk, if it is small enough, or to a writable CD-ROM, or, for that matter, to another hard drive, if you have one.

Once downloaded, open the directory to which it was downloaded. Most software files downloaded will have the extension *exe*, designating that they are *executable* files. Double click the file name, which will activate the installation wizard. Follow the instructions by selecting the *Next* button when prompted. It is easiest to accept the default location for installation of the application. Once the installation is complete, which in some cases necessitates restarting the computer, you can access the application through the *Start* menu.

Some software applications are compressed, usually identifiable by the extension *zip*. To unzip these you need an application called WinZip. Installation and use of this application are beyond the scope of this book.

There are two ways to uninstall applications installed on PCs with Microsoft operating systems. The easiest, and preferred, method is to open the *Start* menu, select *Settings* and then *Control Panel*. This will open a window with various icons in it. Select *Add/Remove Programs*. This opens a window that should list all the programs installed on your machine. Select the program that you want to uninstall and then the button to install/uninstall. This will start the uninstall program. Respond to wizard promptings. Invariably, at the termination of the uninstall process you will see a message that states that not all the files could be removed, and that you need to remove the remainder manually. Don't worry about this. The number of files and their size will be small. In any event, it is rarely the case that the uninstall program removes all the relevant files.

The second way of removing the files associated with programs, which applies especially to those that are not listed in the *Add/Remove Programs* window, is by accessing the folders where the files have been installed and deleting these. You should attempt this only if you are fairly confident that you will not be deleting critical programs inadvertently. In principle the procedure is very simple.

If you have installed the program, as recommended above, in the default location, this will be in a sub-folder of the *Program Files* folder on the operating system drive, invariably the C drive. Open your file manager, *Explorer*, from the *Start* menu and click on the + next to *Local Disk (C)* to reveal the sub-folders. Click on the + to the left of the *Program Files* folder. Select and open the sub-folder with the name of the application that you want to uninstall by right clicking on it. See if there is a file in it called Uninstall. If there is, double click on it, which will activate the uninstall wizard. If not, right click on the folder, select Delete and respond affirmatively to the question whether you want to delete the application. This will remove the folders and its contents to the *Recycle Bin*.

Having deleted the folder including the application, you still have the option of restoring the *status quo ante*. In *Explorer* double click on the *Recycle Bin* icon, locate the folder of the application that you have deleted, right click on it, and select *Restore*. You can, in this way, restore any file that you have deleted from your hard disk. Note that you cannot do this in respect of files that have been deleted from portable media. Also, once you have gone through the uninstall procedure, either by way of the *Control Panel*, or by using the uninstall file in the application folder, you cannot restore the application from the recycle bin. Of course, once you have emptied the *Recycle Bin* there is no possibility of retrieving/restoring the files that were listed there and therefore no possibility that the application will execute.

11.6 Creating a folder

You need a folder on your hard drive to which to download files. If there is a *temp* folder on your hard drive, use this. If not, create one. Open *Explorer*, your file manager, and click on the icon for the C drive. Open the *File* menu and select *New/Folder*. The folder icon will appear at the bottom of the right panel in Explorer, with the default text name, *New Folder*, highlighted in blue and flashing. Type *temp* and hit the Enter key. To rename a folder, right click on it, select the *Rename* option, type the name of the new folder, and hit the Enter key.

11.7 Web references: computers and Internet

How Stuff Works: Computers and Internet

http://www.howstuffworks.com/sc-computers-internet.htm

Provides clearly written explanatory articles on a variety of topics relating to computers and the Internet, such as computer memory, home networking, WebCams, viruses, newsgroups, MP3.

Free Email Address Directory

http://www.emailaddresses.com/

This site provides links to more than 1100 free email services, as well as information on matters connected to email. It is not necessary to restrict your email Internet account to Hotmail. For instance, 020 (*http://mail.020.co.uk/*) provides 5 MB of space, address books, very sophisticated filtering facilities, collection of emails from a number of different POP email services, and many others. This is also a source of information on free email services in other countries and languages.

Webopedia

http://www.webopedia.com/

An excellent online encyclopaedia for computer- and Internet-related terms. Provides concise and clear definitions as well as links to more detailed articles. Search by keyword or by subject. Keyword searching is more efficient in terms of speed. Also includes a reference area, which includes useful information such as country codes, and data formats and their file extensions.

ISPs the list

http://thelist.internet.com/countrycode.html

Links to information on ISP (Internet Service Provider) provision arranged by country. Where available, information includes fees, access type provision (ASDL, ISDN, modem speeds) and contact information. There are separate listings for the USA and Canada.

Note

1. Merrills, J. G. and Robertson A. H., *Human Rights in Europe: A Study of the European Convention on Human Rights*, Manchester: Manchester University Press, 2001, p. 138.

12

Browser features and customisation

As it is highly probable that every reader of this book will have used a browser and be familiar with many aspects of its use, I have refrained from including detailed information on all major aspects of its use. There are, however, certain points that are worth re-emphasising, or broaching, as the case may be.

The two main browsers are Microsoft's Internet Explorer, now available in version 6.X, and Netscape. In point of fact, Netscape is now a suite of programs, which, in addition to the browser, called *Navigator*, includes an HTML editor, called *Composer*, and an email client. If your PC has the requisite system resources, it is worth using the latest versions, which can be downloaded from the Netscape, *http://www.netscape.com*, and Microsoft, *http://www.microsoft.com*, sites.

12.1 Home page

The default Home page for both browsers is set to the developers' Home pages. As it is unlikely that you will want to connect to Microsoft or Netscape each time you use your browser, you should change this to a page that you visit most frequently.

(1) Internet Explorer

On the *Tools* menu select *Internet Options*. On the *General* tab, type the URL of the page you want as your default Home page. You can also select the *Use Blank* option. Selecting the *Use Default* button will restore the URL to the Microsoft Home page.

(2) Netscape

From the *Edit* menu select *Preferences*. In the *Location* dialog box type the URL of the page you want as your default Home page.

12.2 Links toolbar buttons

There are a number of ways to access easily pages that you want to download regularly. (1) If you remember their URLs, you can type these in the *Address/Location* dialog boxes of the two main browsers. (2) You can add them to your *Favorites/Bookmarks* and select these. (3) The third option is to create a button for these on the *Links/Personal* toolbars of IE and Netscape respectively. This last, although it initially takes two minutes per button, is well worth undertaking given the amount of time that it is likely to save. It is probably best to create buttons for the sites that you are likely to visit most frequently.

(1) Internet Explorer

You can create buttons on the Links toolbar, as in Figure 12.1. First, make sure that it is visible by selecting *Toolbars* from the *Edit* menu, and then checking *Links*. There are some default buttons on this toolbar, most of which you may not find useful. You can alter their properties so that when selected you access sites of your choice. Right click on a button and select *Properties*. The button properties dialog box appears, a portion of which is shown in Figure 12.2.

Figure 12.1

Type the name of the site/page you want the button to link to in the text box on the *General* tab. On the *Web Document* tab type in the URL of the page, and then select OK. The name on the button will have changed. When you are online and select the button, it will access the URL that you specified.

There are a number of ways that you can create *additional* buttons. (1) Access the page that you want to create a button linking to. Place the cursor over the

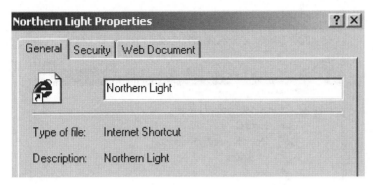

Figure 12.2

small icon that is situated to the left of the URL in the *Address* box, as displayed in Figure 12.3, left click the mouse and press down, then drag the icon to the *Links* bar and release. (2) Drag any link from a page, or from the *Favorites* bar, to the *Links* bar and release. Note that if you create more links on the bar than can be accommodated by your screen size, those that cannot be accommodated will be listed in a drop-down menu, which is accessed by selecting the double arrows at its right.

Figure 12.3

(2) Netscape

You can create buttons on the *Personal Toolbar*, as illustrated in Figure 12.4. Make sure that the toolbar is displayed by checking it from the *Show* option on the *View* menu. If it is still not visible you may need to click on the small arrow at the extreme left of the browser window, below the *Bookmarks* button.

Figure 12.4

To add a button to the toolbar, access the page concerned, select the *Bookmarks* button, and from the menu presented choose *File Bookmark/Personal Bookmark Folder*. To modify button information, or to delete buttons, you need to select *Bookmarks* and choose the *Edit Bookmarks . . .* option, which will open the *Bookmarks* editing window, as in Figure 12.5.

To add a new button, right click on *Personal Toolbar Folder* and select *New Bookmark* from the menu. Fill in the details for the title of the button and the URL, and select the OK button. To delete a button, right click on the bookmark

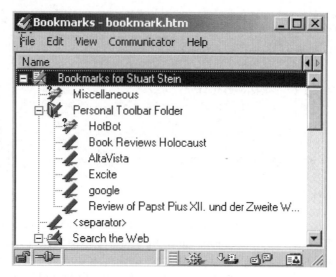

Figure 12.5

(e.g. *AltaVista* in Figure 12.5) and select *Delete*. To modify details, right click on a bookmark, select *Properties*, and modify the details as required, selecting OK to close. When you have finished, close the *Bookmarks* window.

12.3 Adding the Google toolbar to IE

As noted in Chapter 5 (p. 49) Google incorporates some useful features, features that are accessible from a toolbar that you can download and link to your browser, as an additional toolbar. In addition, whenever you want to query Google, all you have to do is type your keywords in its query box, and select the *Search Web* button adjacent to it, which will connect to the search engine, downloading the first page of hits that correspond to your query. This, and the features available on the toolbar, I find to be invaluable.

To install it, access the Google Home page at ***http://www.google.com*** and select the *Google Toolbar* link. Just follow the online instructions, and it will be added to your IE toolbars. Note, if having followed the instructions, you cannot observe it, select the *View* menu, then *Toolbars/Google*.

12.4 Saving files with the browser

1. Most Web pages contain a mixture of text and images. The major difference between IE and Netscape is that when you select *Save As . . .* from the *File* menu, IE will save both text and images, whereas Netscape will save only the text component of the file. Thus, when you later select *Open* from the *File*

menu and load the file into the browser window, the images will be missing. Although, as noted below, there is a way of ensuring that the images can be saved as well, this is a time-consuming and tedious task, the more so the greater the number of images included in a file.

When you save a Web page in IE to disk, the text is saved as an HTML file, say *news.htm*, whereas the images will be saved to a folder named *news_files*. When you load the saved file into the browser window, the images will be loaded from the appropriate folder. If you move the saved file to another directory you must also move the files folder to the same directory if you want the images to load as well when you open the HTML file.

With Netscape, having saved the text by selecting *Save As . . .* from the *File* menu, you need to save all the images (which include image separators, icons, pictures, clipart) by right clicking each with the mouse and choosing *Save Image As . . .* from the menu. You should save the image files to the same directory as that to which you saved the HTML file. This may not entirely overcome the problem because when you load the HTML file into the browser window, whether the images also load depends on where the images were stored relative to the directory of the HTML file on the original server, and on how the links to the file were coded. In many cases the images will load, but in others you will need to recode the HTML file.

Another point to bear in mind is that when you move the HTML file to another storage directory, you will also need to move the images. As there may be many associated with a particular HTML file, you will need to know which of these to select from all those in the directory. To avoid most of these problems, it is recommended that when saving Web pages to disk for future use, you do so with IE.

The comments made above concerning the saving of images in Netscape apply only to HTML files. For others, for instance Word or PDF files, this does not apply as the graphics are embedded in the file, whereas in HTML files the graphics are merely linked to.

2. With both IE and Netscape it is possible to save files without downloading the files into the browser window. In IE right click on the link to the file and select *Save Target As. . . .* With Netscape, click on the hyperlink while simultaneously pressing the Shift key. When doing this with Netscape, bear in mind the comments made in (1) above respecting the saving of images with Netscape.

12.5 Bookmarks/Favorites

Bookmarks in Netscape, named *Favorites* in IE, are hyperlinks to files that are stored on Internet or Intranet servers.[1] Bookmarking is a means of being able to find files that have been considered particularly useful during subsequent online sessions. Systematic bookmarking is essential given the large number of potentially useful sites that are accessible, and the difficulty of remembering for very long, if at all, their addresses.

Although there are certain features associated with Netscape's *Bookmarks* that are not replicable with *Favorites*, in my view it is easier to work with the latter. In any event, it is not worth working with both *Bookmarks* and *Favorites* as sooner or later you will encounter problems of knowing where to find links to particular documents.[2] Instead of synchronising between the two, which takes up time and/or requires additional software, depending on the browser versions that you are using, it is far better to stick to one of the two. It does not take up a lot of time if you find a useful file while using Netscape to copy and paste the URL into the *Address* box of IE, download it, and then add it to *Favorites*; about 20 seconds.

As there are many similarities between the procedures for adding and editing *Bookmarks* and *Favorites*, I will illustrate primarily with reference to the latter. The additional functionality of Netscape's bookmarking facility does not, to my mind, merit discussion here.

There are two methods of accessing *Favorites*: from the *Favorites* menu and from the *Favorites* button, on the standard toolbar. The menu is best used for adding to and organising *Favorites*, the latter, if necessary, for accessing bookmarked sites. When you select the button, a frame with the *Favorites* listed appears on the left, taking up screen space.

The *Favorites* menu will include some default folders and has the appearance of Figure 12.6.

When you access a site that you want to bookmark, select the *Favorites* menu and then *Add to Favorites*. A window that corresponds to Figure 12.7 will appear. Make sure that the title is sufficiently descriptive and, if not, change it. You can

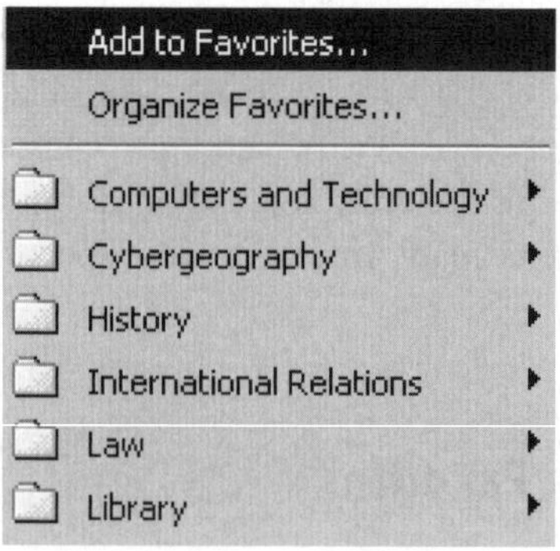

Figure 12.6

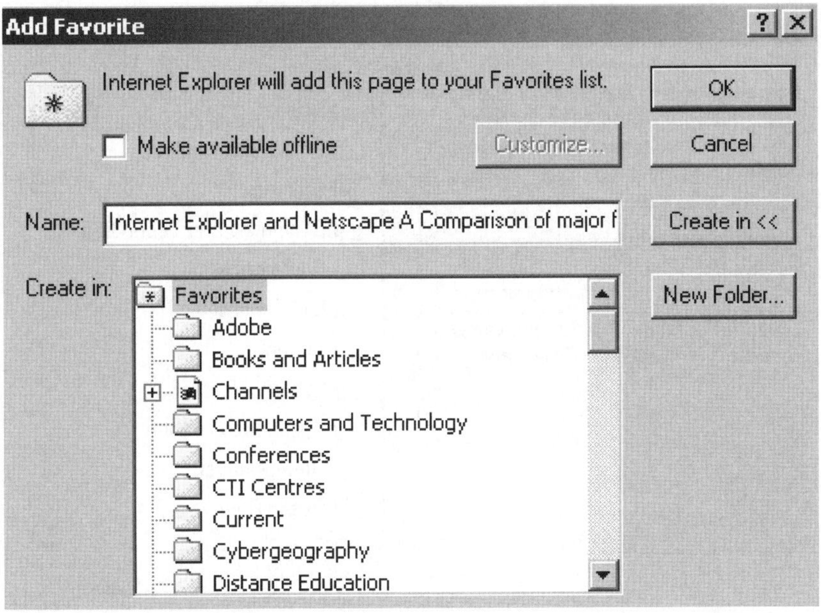

Add Favorite

Internet Explorer will add this page to your Favorites list.

☐ Make available offline

Customize...

OK

Cancel

Name: Internet Explorer and Netscape A Comparison of major f

Create in <<

Create in:

* Favorites
  - Adobe
  - Books and Articles
  + Channels
  - Computers and Technology
  - Conferences
  - CTI Centres
  - Current
  - Cybergeography
  - Distance Education

New Folder...

Figure 12.7

also decide to place the reference to the file in a particular folder. To create a folder, select the button *New Folder*. This will open a dialog box, as illustrated in Figure 12.8. Type in a descriptive name and select OK. Add the link to Favorites by selecting OK again (Figure 12.7).

It is possible to create new folders at any time. However, it is much easier to do this as you go along, and, if necessary, reorganise later, than it is to spend time organising a long list of *Favorites* into folders at some future date. It is advisable to work out, as you go along, what folders you are likely to need. You can always make sub-folders of folders later on, rename them, or delete them,

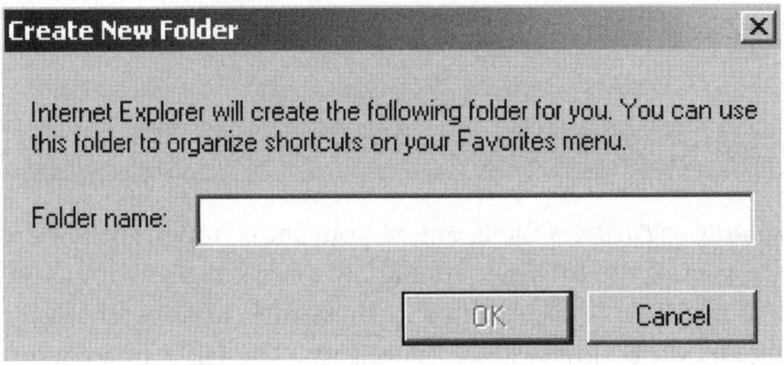

Create New Folder

Internet Explorer will create the following folder for you. You can use this folder to organize shortcuts on your Favorites menu.

Folder name:

OK

Cancel

Figure 12.8

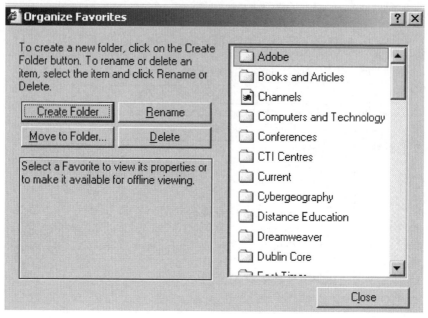

Figure 12.9

having moved the links elsewhere. Make the names as descriptive as possible. Having created folders, when you come to a page that you want to bookmark, select *Create in* . . . (Figure 12.7), to choose the folder in which the link will be included.

By selecting *Favorites/Organize Favorites*, a window corresponding to Figure 12.9 appears, which allows for the creation and deletion of folders, the deletion and renaming of links, and the moving of folders and links.

A folder or link can be renamed by right clicking on it and selecting *Rename* from the menu, or by clicking on and selecting the *Rename* button. To move a link to a folder, or to a different folder, select the link, then the *Move to Folder* . . . button, and choose one from the list. Additional folders can be created by selecting *Create Folder*.[3]

12.6 Saving Bookmarks and Favorites

Your *Bookmarks* or *Favorites* file is one of your most important resources. If you are a serious user of the Internet, after a few years it is likely that you will have hundreds, if not thousands, of links in these files, arranged by topic. Finding them all again will be impossible. Establishing the URLs of some of the most important will take up many hours of research. For these reasons *it is critical to save these files regularly*. If your hard disk is damaged, or the file becomes corrupted for some reason, it will be impossible to retrieve the data. Neither of these are unheard-of events.

There is no point in saving the file to the same disk, or even the same machine, as that on which the original is stored. Moreover, it is desirable to save these files on more than one unit of a storage medium (floppy, hard disk, CD-R/RW or zip drive), and to ensure that they are kept in separate places.

Favorites are stored in a folder of that name. Netscape *Bookmarks* are kept in a file named *bookmark.htm*. The easiest way to locate both, which by default are located on the C drive of most PCs, but not necessarily on laboratory-networked PCs, is to open Microsoft's file management application, Explorer, highlight the C drive, and then use the search facility by selecting the Search button. In the text box *Search for files or folders named:* enter *bookmark.htm* or *favorites*. The file/folder will appear listed in the panel on the right. Right click on this and select *Send to:* and choose to which drive to send the file/folder.

Note: the *Send to:* feature copies the file to the destination chosen; it does not move them. If you are working on a networked computer and cannot trace the files, contact your help desk administrators.

Notes

1. In Netscape it is also possible to bookmark files directly from your hard disk. Select the *Bookmark* button from the toolbar, then *Edit Bookmarks/New Bookmark*, and enter the details of the new bookmark, e.g. Title: *Notes on Lacan*, Location: *c:\Notes\Lacan.doc*, Description: *Whatever*. Close by selecting the OK button. When you select the bookmark in future, a message will appear asking whether you want to save the file to disk or open it. If you select *Open*, the document will open in the application associated with that file extension.

   You cannot do this directly in IE. There is, however, a workaround for some files/applications. If you can open a file in a Microsoft Office application, Word, for instance, you can add it to *Favorites*. First, load the file. In the *View* menu select *Toolbars/Web* (if this is not open already). Select *Favorites* from the toolbar, and then *Add to Favorites*. If you want to store this in a particular folder, select it.

   The *Favorites* file is common to all applications on the machine, so if you are subsequently working with the IE browser, or another Office application (Access, Excel, Outlook, PowerPoint), the file will appear in the *Favorites* list in all of these. You could, for instance, add a link to the Inbox in Outlook, so that when working with another application, if you select it Outlook will open, without having to select the icon from the Desktop, or Programs.

2. There are applications that synchronise Netscape *Bookmarks* with Internet Explorer Favorites. Their use is beyond the scope of this book. One such application is SyncURLs, available from *the ZDNet Software Library*, **http://www.zdnet.com/** (or conduct a search with the name as the query term). In versions 4.X of IE there is a facility for importing Netscape *Bookmarks*, but only one at a time. In Versions 5.X and above, there is an import/export wizard that allows the importing of the Netscape *Bookmark* file,

but which will, of course, include only those attributes of the bookmarks that are compatible with *Favorites*.

3. You can also rename and delete links and folders in Microsoft's file management system Explorer. It is easier and faster to do it in Explorer than with the *Organize Favorites* feature. Locate the *Favorites* folder (see section 12.6), right click on folders or links, and rename, and delete as appropriate. You can create a new folder in the usual way by selecting *New/Folder* from the *File* menu, and you can move links from one folder to another through drag and drop.

Glossary

The terms included below are those that crop up relatively frequently in the context of Internet- and PC-related work. I have included some that have not been mentioned in the text. Also, when appropriate, I have provided the common/colloquial interpretation or use of the term rather than the technical.
Items in brackets at the end of an entry signify main or related entries.

Algorithm 'A formula or set of steps for solving a particular problem. To be an algorithm, a set of rules must be unambiguous and have a clear stopping point. Algorithms can be expressed in any language, from natural languages such as English or French to [computer] programming languages.' (Source: Webopedia)

Applet A program created with the Java programming language that can be embedded in a Web (HTML) page, and downloaded in browsers that are Java enabled, that is, browsers that can read Java. Java programs are cross-platform, which means that if embedded in a Web page they will work on all operating systems (Windows, Unix, Macintosh, etc.). For security and other reasons, some system administrators disable the Java functionality of browsers used on their networks. (JAVA)

ASCII (American Standard Code for Information Interchange) Also known as ISO 646. This is a universally accepted standard for the encoding of character data in binary digits to represent letters of the alphabet, punctuation, digits, a few symbols (e.g. $ and &), and some control characters. The aim was to create a format for information exchange that was stripped down to bare essentials, making it readable on virtually all computing platforms and editors. If you take any file created in a word-processing package, for instance Word or WordPerfect, and save it in ASCII format, all the embedded codes will be stripped out (columns, bold, italics, tables, etc.).

Bandwidth A term used to refer to the volume of data that can be moved per unit of time over a network. When bandwidth is low, the download time is extended relative to that of when it is high.

Baud A unit that measures the volume of data transmitted per second between a modem and some hardware component, such as a PC or a server. Modems with higher baud rates transmit data faster than those with lower ones. At present the most commonly sold modems have baud ratings of 56,600 bps.

Boolean operators Named after the nineteenth-century British mathematician George Boole. In computer programming terms they are operators that permit true or false responses. In Internet work they are employed in search engine queries and include the operators AND, OR, AND NOT.

Browser A shortening of Web Browser, originally used to designate an application that could be used to *read* pages compiled in HTML format, or Web pages.

Byte A byte is a group of bits that constitute a unit of information. In computing terms a byte consists of eight *bits*, which together represent a discrete unit of information, such as a letter, a number, or special character or symbol. When you are downloading files from the Internet the number of bytes that have been downloaded relative to the total is indicated in the status bar of the browser, if this is visible. The size of software applications and storage media are represented in terms of bytes. (KILOBYTE, MEGABYTE, GIGABYTE)

Client A computer program or process that issues commands to another computer or program. A Web browser, for instance, is a client of a Web server. The browser issues commands to the server requiring it to download data. Similarly, an FTP application is a client of an FTP server. (CLIENT–SERVER COMPUTING)

Client–server computing In distributed computing one part of the framework for distributing data between computers is the client, through which commands are issued to the other component, the server. An FTP (File Transfer Protocol) client, for instance, issues a request to an FTP server to display its directory hierarchy, and, subsequently, to download (send) a requested file. The server responds by displaying the directory structure (folders/files) and by downloading the file requested.

Cookie The term *cookie* is employed to refer to information that is transmitted by the server from which you have downloaded a file/page to your computer. This is stored on your computer, and activated when you subsequently access the same page – or sometimes other pages on the same site – to transmit/ retransmit information about yourself or your preferences, to the server.

Digital Any thing or event that is expressible in terms of the integers 0 or 1, or fixed states, on/off. (Source: PC Lexicon)

Directory (Folder) Technically, a block of data relating to a particular drive in which links to files are stored. Frequently the files relate to a similar application, topic, or procedure. In Windows 95+ and NT+ they are referred to as folders rather than directories. In current usage the two terms are interchangeable.

FAQ (Frequently Asked Questions) A FAQ is a list of questions that are most frequently asked by users concerning a particular subject, along with appropriate replies to them.

File path The file path is used to describe the location of a file on a computer storage device. The absolute directory path specifies the location of a file in terms of the drive and folders that need to be opened to get to it on the computer on which it is located.

File server Refers to the computer on a network on which are stored files and programs to be used by workstations connected to it. This computer, being a dedicated file server with a fast, high-capacity hard disk, expedites the handling of files.

Firewall A damage-prevention and security system usually employed by organisations connected to the Internet. It consists of code which aliases, hides, or blocks the computer shielded by it from identification by any other computer on the network. Well-constructed firewalls prevent those who do not have legitimate access to the network from tampering with files and systems on it, or from downloading files to which there are no anonymous public access rights.

Freeware Software applications for which no payment need be made while allowing their authors to retain copyright over them.

FTP (File Transfer Protocol) A protocol used to transfer files from one network-connected host to another. There are specialised software applications, FTP clients, that can be used to accomplish such transfers from dedicated FTP servers.

FYI Stands for (For Your Information.)

GIF (Graphics Interchange Format) A file format used for displaying and distributing graphics images over the World Wide Web.

Gigabyte One thousand million bytes. (BYTE)

Hits Refers to the number of entries included in a database that relate to a query entered by a user searching it.

Home page Generally used to refer to the introductory page of a Web presentation, the one to which all other pages are linked, which, in turn, usually link back to it.

Host A computer on a network that, with the assistance of compatible software, can communicate with other computers on the network. Some authorities appear to confuse the term host with that of node, interpreting the former as designating any computer linked to the Internet.

HTML (Hypertext Markup Language) A structural markup language that indicates to specialised software applications that can *read* it (Web browsers, for instance) how the text, graphic images, and video and audio files associated with it are to be displayed. HTML is concerned principally with the structure of documents, rather than with their appearance. HTML is under constant revision by the Internet Engineering Task Force (IETF), as well as by browser developers.

HTTP (Hypertext Transport Protocol) 'A protocol for transferring data formats between a server and client. Data formats include plain text, hypertext, images, sound, public or proprietary formats specified as MIME type, and metainformation about the data.' (Source: R. Darnell *et al.*, *HTML 4 Unleashed*, 1997)

Hyperlink A method of linking from one file to another by selecting a segment of text in the file (the hyperlink), which, under normal conditions, downloads the file pointed to. In Web pages, the segment that constitutes the hyperlink is usually differentiated from the surrounding text by its colour, and by being underlined, although this need not be so. Although hyperlinks are associated by most people primarily with Web documents, there are many software applications that employ hyperlinks as a means of moving from one section of a document to another (e.g. Word, Adobe Exchange).

Hypertext Invented in the mid-1960s by Douglas Engelbert. 'The practical and conceptual heart of the Web, hypertext is a system of relating points within and outside a text to each other nonlinearly. Hypertext, as manifested with hyperlinks, moves a user from text to text at will.' (Source: R. Darnell *et al.*, *HTML 4 Unleashed*, 1997.) As it is possible to hyperlink through graphics as well, it is currently becoming common to subsume hypertext under hypermedia.

Interface Refers to the front-ends of software applications, that is, the combination of windows, toolbars, icons, etc., that appear once the application is launched. Accordingly, a user might refer to the fact that the Netscape interface is more user-friendly (intuitive) than that of Adobe's Photoshop.

Internet Protocol (IP) Part of the TCP/IP suite of protocols that governs data exchanges across the Internet.

Internet Service Provider Generic term that covers private companies providing Internet connectivity and additional online services to users, usually in return for a monthly subscription fee. These additional services might include email accounts and facilities, access to newsgroups, discussion boards, and Web space.

IP address This is the address that uniquely identifies a particular computer (node) on the Internet. Every computer linked to the Internet needs a unique address so that data can be transmitted to and from it. The IP address is expressed in numerical terms, e.g. 158.152.1.122. Most IP addresses have corresponding domain name addresses, such as microsoft.com.

Java A programming language developed by Sun Microsystems. The early versions were distributed in the public domain in 1995. The technical definition is somewhat complex and unlikely to be of much interest to most readers of this book. In practical terms the promise of Java is to deliver executable content over the Internet through Web browsers that are Java enabled; that is, through Web pages that can download Java applets. By executable content is meant software applications. In principle, therefore, instead of a word processor being installed on the hard disk of your PC, it could be downloaded to your PC as a Java program. (APPLET)

JPEG (Joint Photographic Experts Group Format) One of the most popular graphics file formats used to display images on the Web.

Kilobyte One thousand bytes. (BYTE)

LISTSERV An abbreviation of LIST SERVer. A proprietary software program that stores a list of electronic mail addresses and that can execute various commands associated with the management of mailing lists.

Mailing list Subject-based discussion groups implemented through electronic mail, most commonly with the assistance of software programs that automate many of the tasks associated with mailing list management tasks. (LISTSERV)

Megabyte One million bytes. (BYTE)

Newsgroup See USENET

NNTP (Network News Transfer Protocol) The protocol used for distribution and retrieval of data relating to news groups. (USENET)

Node Generally used to refer to any computer reachable over a network, including the Internet. Each computer that satisfies this condition is said to be a node on the network concerned.

Operating System (OS) 'Operating systems are the programs or collections of programs which act as translators between a computer's processing chips and programs designed to run on them. . . . Examples of operating systems are

DOS, Windows, OS/2, UNIX, and Macintosh's System/Finder.' (Source: PC Lexicon)

PDF (Portable Document Format) A document format developed by Adobe Inc. PDF files are cross-platform, which means that they can be read on any computer, irrespective of the operating system that it is using. In order to read PDF files you need to have the special Adobe Acrobat Reader. This is available as freeware, and can be downloaded from the Adobe Home page at *http://www.adobe.com*. As many documents accessible over the Internet are in this format it is well worth installing the reader, if it is not already available. The most recent versions of the main browsers incorporate it. To write documents in PDF format you need to purchase the appropriate software from Adobe, particulars of which are available on its site.

Plugin In the context of browser-use, the term applies to a software application that is not part of its original build, but that can be *attached* to it, thereby extending its features, usually so that file formats that otherwise would not be viewable through it, are, such as certain audio or video files.

Protocol Protocols are established international standards that specify details relating to how computers will interact with each other in relation to the exchange of commands and data governing specific applications and/or procedures.

Retrieval algorithm The algorithm used by the *retrieval engine* to select results to be displayed in response to queries that have been submitted to its database. See ALGORITHM.

Retrieval engine The software program that interrogates a search engine's database and delivers matching results.

Search engine In Internet parlance, the front-end of a large database containing information relating to files (text, graphic, video, audio, software – and combinations thereof) accessible from Internet-connected servers. They vary in their breadth of coverage of Internet resources, their speed of retrieval of information, and the sophistication of the query syntax that can be employed to track down resources indexed in their databases.

Server Used to refer both to a piece of hardware that performs the task of providing specified resources (for instance, a file or printer server), and the server software component in client–server applications, such as Netscape Web Server and Microsoft Peer Web Server. (FILE SERVER, CLIENT–SERVER COMPUTING)

Shareware A system of software distribution whereby the user is afforded a trial period to experience the software, usually 30 days, prior to being required to pay for its continuing use. The author retains copyright throughout. Much contemporary shareware invariably incorporates coding that prevents use after the *trial* period has expired, thus negating somewhat the difference between it and proprietary software.

SMTP (Simple Mail Transfer Protocol) A protocol that is used for transferring electronic mail between computers.

TCP (Transmission Control Protocol) One of the suite of protocols that is central to the functioning of the Internet, concerned principally with the accurate transmission of data between Internet-linked computers.

URL (Uniform Resource Locator) An Internet address. These have standardised formats. The URL specifies the type of Internet service that is being accessed (World Wide Web, FTP, etc.), and the file path of the resource being sought. The URL is the entry that is inserted in the *location/go* box in a browser.

Usenet Generically used to designate the network of tens of thousands of newsgroups that are arranged into different subject hierarchies and topics. The software programs that manage newsgroup communications rely on a specific protocol, the NNTP (Network News Transfer Protocol).

Wild Card Commonly specified by * or ? in Windows and DOS operating systems, it is used in searches for information or files, and in copying, moving, filtering, and backing up files. Most Internet search engines allow for the use of wild cards in their query syntax.

World Wide Web A hypertext-based distributed information system developed by Tim Berners Lee at CERN, the European Centre for Particle Physics. CERN was responsible for developing the early standards for the Web and the first command-based Web browser.

Index